Barefoot Boy

A Year in the Life of a 1930s Farm Boy

Raymond Schairer

With Foreword by Sandor Slomovits

LittleLight Publishing

Published by:

LittleLight Publishing
2000 Penncraft Ct.
Ann Arbor, MI

For more information:
BarefootBoyBook.com
sandor2021@gmail.com
(734) 665-0165

Printed in the United States of America
First published July 2008
Second Edition October 2010

Text set in Adobe Caslon Pro
Design by Daniel Slomovits

Library of Congress Control Number: 2008930559

ISBN#: 978-0-9675933-5-7

I want to thank everyone who helped me in the creation of this book.

I met Reverend Charles Cookingham in 2003, when I joined the creative writing group he was leading in the Chelsea Retirement Center. He was the one who got me started writing these memoirs.

Miss Josephine Crocker, my English teacher in my years at Dexter High School, 1935-1939, was the first one to encourage my writing.

Sandor Slomovits transcribed my handwritten pages, edited and helped pull this manuscript together. I couldn't have done it without him.

Chris Lord read the final draft and made many helpful editorial suggestions.

Daniel Slomovits, young graphic designer and computer wizard that he is, designed the book and put the manuscript into the format the printers needed.

Rod Knieper, a long time family friend, oversaw the first printing of this book at Bookmasters.

Finally, I want to thank my wife Jane, my lifelong partner. We lived happily ever after.

Foreword

I met Ray Schairer in 1977, when I was learning to play the "bones" from his friend, Percy Danforth. (More on that later.) Our paths crossed occasionally for the next twenty-five years. Then in the fall of 2002 I called him and asked if he would help me with a woodworking project. I wanted to build a music stand for my young daughter, Emily, who was learning to play the violin. I had neither the tools, nor the experience to make one by myself. Ray immediately agreed to help me and out of the process of working together on that project grew one of the warmest, most special friendships of my life. Ray was 80 years old at the time, I was 53 and our friendship had elements of both a father-son and a mentor-student relationship. I began visiting him weekly and we'd work in his shop, making wooden "bones" and other woodworking projects.

Soon after I started working with Ray, I learned that he was in a writing group at the Chelsea Retirement Community where he was living. I asked him to show me the stories he was writing. The book you hold in your hands now are those stories. They are Ray's memories of one year of his childhood.

But first, a very brief biography of Ray and his wife Jane.

They met in the summer of 1946 on a blind date that lasted a week. Jane had been hearing about Ray for some time from her dad, Carl Schlosser, a retired farmer who worked at the Dexter Cooperative, a grain elevator and mill. "He would come home and tell me about this fellow that came in to have feed ground for his cattle, but I wasn't really interested. I'd grown up on a farm. I knew what farming was like and what an unreliable kind of occupation it can be as far as steady income is concerned."

Not that she was waiting for a husband to support her. She was teaching at a rural school near Chelsea, similar to the one she had attended as a child. In the evenings and summers she took classes at Michigan State Normal College, now Eastern Michigan University, to complete her college degree.

Jane, Harold and Helen Sias, on that first, fateful vacation up North.

Ray and Jane finally met when Jane and her friend, Helen Sias, planned a vacation together to Michigan's Upper Peninsula. Helen, a fellow teacher at the rural school had been, fifteen years earlier, Jane's "beginner" or kindergarten teacher, and was now also studying at the Normal College.

At the same time that the two women were making their plans, Ray and Helen's brother Harold, neighbors who sometimes helped each other with farming tasks, were planning a similar vacation.

Somehow, by now neither Ray nor Jane remember how, it was decided they would all go together.

A radical decision for the times, Jane recalls. "I was living on campus that summer and called home to explain to my mother that there had been a change in plans and the four of us would be going together. I still remember her saying, 'Well, you ought to be old enough to know what you're doing.'"

The week long vacation was uneventful and Ray and Jane didn't see each other for nearly a year after, when Ray suddenly showed up at Jane's parents' house one spring evening. She opened the door and greeted him with, "Ray Schairer, what are you doing here?"

Jane's dad was sitting nearby in a rocking chair that night and later told her many times, "I'd have never come back if I'd have been him." But come back he did and they dated for the next three and a half years. Early on in their courtship Ray informed Jane, "I just want you to know that I really don't ever plan on getting married, so if that is what you have in mind, we might as well call it quits right now."

Now, more than sixty years later, they both still laugh with delight at the memory. "Those were fighting words," Jane says. "And I took the challenge!" They married in September of 1950 and built a home around the corner from the house Ray grew up in, where his parents were still living.

Jane and I on our wedding day.

Ray, the third generation of Schairers to farm land near the corner of Jackson and Parker roads west of Ann Arbor, continued running the 120-acre family farm along with his dad. They planted grains, milked cattle, raised sheep and chickens — doing what used to be called general farming.

Jane meanwhile, was still teaching in the Chelsea village school. "That was a new idea, for farmers' wives to continue working after they were married. I can remember how we practiced what we would say to our parents. We felt this would come as somewhat of a surprise to them. Our parents were extra-ordinary I think, as I look back on them and on our friends and some of the kinds of problems they had with their parents. Ours just kind of took in stride what we did. And if they had some doubts, they never let us know."

After teaching for ten years and completing her college degree, a new opportunity came up for Jane. Some of her friends in the United Methodist Church of Chelsea were forming a cooperative nursery school, the precursor of today's day care centers, and they asked Jane to help organize it. "The first year, we were on the third floor of the village government building in Chelsea. The fire station was in the same building. Every time the fire engines went out when school was in progress we would all run to the windows and watch them leave."

In the mid Fifties many of the village schools were beginning to consolidate and to bus children from the rural areas. So the following year, the nursery school was able to buy—for one dollar—a small rural school from the Chelsea school system. During the ten years Jane taught there, the program went from two half days to two full days and an extra afternoon.

The actor Jeff Daniels is the most famous of her ex-students. "But even today, I'll read about people in the local newspaper and I'll say 'Oh, that's one of my kids'." Ray and Jane still run into Jeff Daniels occasionally and Ray laughs as he recalls telling Jeff one time, "The best thing I ever saw you do was when you played Tevye in Fiddler on the Roof when you were a senior in high school."

Somewhere along the way Ray and Jane decided not to have children. "We were so busy and I think we thought we'd have them later, and then that didn't quite work out. We considered adoption but Ray didn't think that was the best route to go. Finally we just decided we wouldn't do it."

But they continued to be very involved with children and education. Jane, in addition to her work at the nursery school also did volunteer work with church youth groups.

"I had an office in the local Methodist Women's Society of Christian Service and we filled out reports on what we were doing. And I could fill out those reports, make them quite lengthy, and make it look like we were doing a horrible amount of work in the Chelsea church. And we were doing some really good things with the youth at that point—and have to this day." Eventually, in 1973 she became

President of the United Methodist Women's Organization, which co-ordinated the activities of local groups throughout the eastern half of Michigan's Lower Peninsula and the entire Upper Peninsula. She also became the first lay woman elected to lead the Church's General Conference delegation and the first to serve as Conference Secretary.

When her four-year term expired she accepted the position of Christian Education Director at the Chelsea Church. She held that position for more than seventeen years and worked with all age groups—infants to adults; coordinating classes, the library, a summer camp program and the work of more than a hundred volunteers every year. "The church has been good to me," she says gratefully. "I have been able to travel and go to so many places I never would have gone to if it weren't for my work."

Although Ray's primary occupation for most of his life has been farming, he has also taught children. For over fifty years he spent many Saturday afternoons in his workshop, teaching woodworking skills to boys and girls in the local 4-H program.

Like Jane, he keeps track of his former students. "They come up to me on the street sometimes and say, 'You got me off to the right start. I just built my own house.' Over the years I've had a number of these fellows tell me that what they're doing now, is related to what they learned in my workshop. And they sent their kids back to me. I've taught two generations."

Ray's workshop was a converted chicken coop he built using mostly recycled materials. When, in the mid Fifties, the Whitney Theater on North Main Street in Ann Arbor was being torn down, Ray and a friend of his hitched wagons to their tractors and drove to the site. "I had seen movies at that theater when it was up and running. We loaded up two by fours, plywood and all sorts of stuff and hauled it back to the farm. You can't do that any more. You have to build using all new materials. The old stuff goes to the dump." One of the interior walls of his workshop was paneled with a big plywood sign that was used to advertise "King Kong" when it had first shown at the theater.

It was Ray's woodworking skills that got him involved in one of the longest friendships and business relationships of his life. In 1976 Percy Danforth, Ann Arbor's internationally recognized "bones" virtuoso, came to Ray and asked him to make instruments for his students.

The "bones" are two pieces of wood, each about seven inches long, an inch wide and slightly curved, in the shape of rib bones. They are percussion instruments that sound similar to castanets and get their name from the curved animal bones that people played originally. They are considered among the oldest musical instruments played by human beings. There are drawings on the pyramids of Egypt depicting people playing the bones; they are mentioned in Shakespeare's plays, and in the U.S. they were widely used in the vaudeville and minstrel shows popular in the late 19th century.

Percy Danforth playing the bones.

Percy learned to play the bones as a child in the early 1900s, and played them as a hobby all his life. In the 1970s he began playing the bones in a few public performances, and word of the unusual instruments spread. Soon Percy found himself teaching many students and needed instruments for them. He turned to Ray, who began crafting bones for him. Ray estimates that since 1976 he has made well over fifty thousand pairs of bones. He still uses as his template the original piece of wood that Percy brought him, to show how he wanted the bones shaped.

Making music has also been a lifelong passion for Ray. He has played piano since his teen years. "My grandmother bought the piano that I still play for my dad when he was six years old. We had a trio, my dad, sister and I. He played the violin and my sister played the saxophone. As long as I was accompanying them I could get away with it. But I didn't want to be up there as a soloist. We played all sorts of places. In Chelsea the Kiwanis club used to put on shows, and between acts they'd get us to come up and play a little. Things like that."

Being a farmer didn't leave him very much time for playing, but since he's been retired he's been playing more. For a number of years, before he and Jane moved from their home, he played for people living in the Chelsea Retirement Center. "I played a little for them during the dinner hour once in a while. Just background music. I play some of the old time hymns and that's what these elderly folks like. I tell them, 'I'm not the best piano player' and they say, 'Oh but you play what we like to hear.' And it's great therapy for my fingers." Today, he and Jane live in the CRC and Ray still plays regularly during church services and other occasions.

Ray and Jane have lived full, rich lives and have left their mark on their community. They have earned the respect and gratitude of three generations of people they have taught, guided and served.

Introduction

I am 81 years old, at an age where I like to reminisce. I used to talk to the Lord and the birds and the animals all day when I farmed. Now I talk to people. Though I still keep quite busy, I have more time to think back and remember events and stories from my long life. Sometimes a conversation sparks a memory, sometimes something I read reminds me of my youth.

I grew up on a farm, near the one that was founded by my great grandfather, John Schairer, who was born in Durweiller, Germany in 1825 and immigrated to America as a young boy with his mother, Anna Maria and his stepfather John Jacob Jedele. (His father, Michael Schairer, died when John was a year old and his mother remarried.) The family was part of the first wave of German immigrants who came to the United States in the late 1820s, and were among the first Germans to settle near Ann Arbor, Michigan.

My great grandfather married Rosina Meyer in 1854. My grandfather, F. Jacob, who was born in 1861, was the fourth of their eleven children. He married my grandmother, Lizabeta Huss, in 1887. My father, Arthur, was born a year later, in 1888, and his brother Herbert, my uncle, was born in 1896.

I was born in 1922 and farmed with my father from the time I graduated high school in 1939 till I retired. Our eighty acre farm, located in Section 19 of Scio Township in Washtenaw County, on the corner of Parker and US-12 (now Jackson Road), is part of the land that my grandparents farmed, and which my father acquired when my grandfather retired. When I began farming with my dad we didn't have a tractor. All our farming tools, plows, cultivators, manure spreaders, were pulled by horses. By the time I retired I was doing all my farming with tractors and combines.

It is now, as I begin to write these stories, a February evening in the year 2003. I am sitting in my easy chair, looking through a book of poems, "The Barefoot Boy," by John Greenleaf Whittier. I come across the words, "Barefoot boy with cheek of tan." And suddenly, I am transported back in time, more than seventy years. Then, I was a typical barefoot boy with cheek of tan, and faded yellow curly hair. And of course, bib overalls! I'm glad I lived in the times I did.

Chapter One

It was 1932, the middle of the Great Depression and also the Dust Bowl days in the West that affected farmers even here in Michigan. We didn't irrigate then. We just accepted the weather that nature gave us. The yields were much less in those years. The wheat grew hardly high enough to cut with a grain binder. The corn got no taller than five feet, and some years only knee high, and then it didn't have any grain on it at all. The farmers would cut that and save the stalks for feed for the sheep and cattle in the winter. The drought hurt us, but not like it did farmers out west.

I was ten that year. It was early June and school was over for the summer. Country School ended right after Memorial Day in those days. It used to end even earlier, at the beginning of May, so kids could help with the planting, but that was before my time. I looked forward to the freedom before me—especially to going barefoot again. I never wore shoes during the summer then, except when we went to church. We just didn't go much of any place else in those days. Neighboring farms were far away, half mile or mile was the closest. The men got together to help each other with farm chores, but we kids rarely saw our school friends during the summer.

On a farm there were chores even a ten year old boy was asked to do. One of my tasks was to get the cows from the pasture for the evening milking. The pasture field was as far away from the barn as could be, almost half a mile. Every late afternoon I would head across the barn yard to the lane that led to our wood lot, next to the pasture field.

I can see it now, as though it was yesterday.

****

I open the gate leading into the lane and start on my way. The path I follow has been used by the cows every day for a long time. The weather has been hot and dry, and the cows' hooves have churned the good earth into deep layers of dust. The feeling, as my bare feet sink in and the dust oozes up between my toes, is almost ecstasy. It's like walking on a soft, warm, sandy beach, or burying my hands in soft flour when I help make bread. On rainy days it was a different feeling, still wonderful, the mud squeezing up between my toes. But this was the drought years. We didn't have a lot of rain those summers.

Sometimes, I step into fresh cow manure in my bare feet. It's not a big deal, though. I just go to the well house, run water on my feet and dry them off in the grass. But there is no stepping into cow manure today. Just the fabulous feeling of my feet sinking into the dust.

A little further down the path my ecstasy is broken by the shrill cry of a killdeer protecting her nest. To the left of the lane is a cornfield planted a few weeks ago and the corn stalks are just forming their leaves. It's a perfect place for the killdeer to make her nest on a little pile of pebbles, hidden under the sheltering leaves. I stop for a moment, assure her I will do her no harm, and continue on my way.

To the right of the lane is a hay field with clover and timothy waving in the summer breeze. The clover is beautiful with bright red blossoms, and the fragrance is unbelievable. I can almost smell the honey the bees will make from it. I keep walking and hear the sound of a bobolink. I find her perched at the edge of her nest, clinging to a tall weed amongst the clover. I start whistling, imitating her call. She's evidently not impressed with my attempt to answer her and flies across the field. I continue on my way, soothing my feet in the wonderful dusty path.

There is a meadow lark flying up ahead of me. He has yellow, white and black markings. Continuing to whistle, I catch the sound of a big old robin. He is perched on top of a fence post near the end of the lane, and it seems as if he's answering my call.

Aerial View of our Farm. I took this picture sometime in the 1940s from the rear cockpit of an open biplane.

I have now reached the highest point along the way. From here I can see almost our whole farm. To the south is our big, hip roof barn, chicken coop, windmill and well house. Past them the trolley tracks run along Old U.S. 12, a two lane highway that was then the main road between Detroit and Chicago. Looking west I see my favorite big elm tree, our orchard and our new farm house. I can look across the corn field, and the hay field next to it, all the way to the big oak trees lining Parker Road. Their fresh new green leaves wave in the breeze. To the east is the timothy and clover field and to the north is the wood lot and past it, the pasture lot, where the cows are.

The lane leads to the wood lot and I skip along the path, stirring up the dust. I look up into the sky and spot two big turkey buzzards cavorting under the late afternoon clouds. I stick my arms straight out at my sides, and skip along, flapping my hands, I feel as if I am about to lift off to join them. Just then a crow lets out a raucous warning call from the top of a tree at the edge of the woods. That brings me back to reality and reminds me why I am here. I look over to the pasture field and see the cows grazing peacefully. I call to them, across the corn field, with my high pitched voice. "Com-boss, com-boss." One of them hears me, raises her head, and looks my way. She answers back, the rest of the herd look at her, and all fifteen of them start for the wood lot on their journey to the barn.

While I wait at the end of the lane for the cows to come out of the woods I lean against the wire farm fence next to the hay field. I hear the dainty song of a bluebird. Her nest is in the old hollow post at the end of the lane. A woodpecker has made a hole in that post, big enough for the bluebird to make a home.

Here come the cows out of the woods, and just ahead of them a rabbit bounds into the lane. When he sees me he turns sharply and hops into the hay field. I am still leaning against the fence as the cows come by single file, kicking up the dry ground with their hooves. One young heifer pulls out of line to come over and nose at me, making sure I am who I am, and then continues on her way. I follow along, wriggling my toes in the deep, dusty, dry dirt all the way back.

The cows know where to go. They file into the barn-yard and I drag the big, heavy, wooden gate across the lane behind them and secure it with a loop of rope hang-ing on the post. Then I head across the barn yard, past the barn, the chicken coop, well house and windmill and into our farmhouse. It's time for supper.

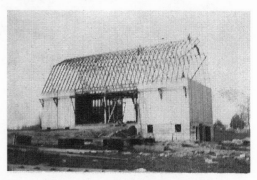

Our barn under construction, circa 1917–18. Our first one was destroyed by a cyclone soon after it was completed.

Father and Mother, my sister Marjorie and little brother Lloyd and I gather around the table and Mother serves us big helpings of ham from the pig we butchered last fall, and home grown mashed potatoes. And, of course, milk. We all dig in. Except for Lloyd who, as usual, is playing with his food, making castles out of the mashed potatoes instead of eating. Mother tells him, "You gotta clean your plate, or you won't get any desert." That gets him going and Mother serves us some strawberries, fresh from the garden. Delicious.

Then, while Mother does the dishes and gets Lloyd ready for bed, Marjorie and I play hide and seek out in the yard and around the house while Father milks the cows.

Then it's one final chore. I meet Father at the well house to help him cool the milk. We use water from our

My father, Arthur, me, Marjorie, Lloyd, and my mother, Anna. July 1930

well to cool the milk from the cows before it's sent to the dairy plant for bottling. Our thirty foot well, near the trolley tracks and the driveway leading to the highway, provides all the water for our homestead. Above the well stands a tall windmill and the wheel is connected to the well pump handle. If there is wind, the windmill pumps the water for us. When there is no wind though, we disconnect the pump handle from the windmill and pump by hand. That's my job.

The water runs in a pipe from the well to the well house and then into a water tank where the milk cans, containing some ninety pounds of milk each, are placed for cooling. For the milk to cool properly, it has to be stirred frequently for about an hour to reach the required sixty degrees. It's not a bad job if the wind blows and the windmill pumps the water. But, on days when there is no wind, I need to do more than just stir. I have to hurry to the base of the windmill, pump cool water into the tank, then run back and stir. Then it's back to the windmill to pump some more water.

Tonight there is a breeze, so I don't have to pump, just stir. The stirrer is a two foot long metal rod with a curved handle on top and a saucer shaped bottom piece, with holes in it. I lift it up and down in the milk can to stir the milk.

When the milk is cool, my chores are done. I head back to the house for one of my favorite evening pastimes, listening to the radio. Marjorie and I pull our chairs up close to the big, tube set that sits on a small table in our downstairs hallway. My cousin Alfred (who we all call Boyce), Aunt Martha's son, built that radio for our family this year. It's the first radio we've ever had. It runs on a six volt car battery.

Some nights Father and Mother listen to Lowell Thomas reading the news, but almost every night at seven Marjorie and I tune in either Detroit's WWJ, or Chicago's WGN and follow the adventures of "Amos and Andy" and laugh. They're funny.

After the fifteen minute show, Mother reminds us it's time to wash up and head upstairs to bed. I watch the sunset from my west window and fall asleep to the sounds of the birds and the frogs down by the creek.

Chapter Two

I wake to the chirping and twittering of birds in the old elm tree. The chickens are cackling and the cows are mooing in the barn yard. Father has begun getting everything ready for the morning milking and I help him pour ground feed into the troughs in the mangers, where the cows are tied up to be milked. Then, while he's milking, I help Mother feed the chickens. We pour a mixture of ground wheat and corn in the long troughs on the floor of the chicken coop. After we're done, I run to the well house and pull the empty milk cart to the barn. When Father has finished milking, he pours each pail of milk through a funnel-shaped strainer, into the big, ten-gallon milk can, then lifts the can into the cart. Together, we push the cart back to the well house. When there's a full can of milk in the cart it's too heavy for me to manage by myself.

It's another hot, dry day. No wind this morning. So, while Father lifts the milk can from the cart, carries it into the well house and lowers it into the cooling tank, I run and disconnect the pump handle from the windmill and pump water from our well into the tank. Then I sprint back to the well house, stir the milk for awhile and run back to the well under the windmill to pump some more cold water. I keep repeating this until the milk has cooled to the required sixty degrees.

Then it's time for breakfast. Some mornings it's oatmeal with milk. Today it's scrambled eggs and Mother's homemade bread, toasted, with butter and honey.

Our farm. There's the windmill on the right.

Halfway through breakfast, we hear the Inter Urban electric trolley bell ring as it goes by our house to the intersection of US-12 and Parker roads, heading west to Jackson. There is very little auto traffic on the two lane road, even though it's the main highway between Detroit and Chicago.

After breakfast it's time for the milk man to come. We are among the last farms on his route. I watch for him impatiently, looking across to Parker Road, to the south, until I finally see him coming our way. He turns onto the highway and stops his 1928 Model A Ford truck in our driveway where Father and I meet him with the milk cart loaded with both cans of milk. The milk man takes down two empty cans from his truck, then he lifts the two full cans of milk from our cart onto the deck of the truck. I watch in awe as grabs the handles on either side, near the top, and lifts those full, ten gallon cans of milk straight up onto the truck. Father says they weigh nearly a hundred pounds each. The truck's deck is higher than I am tall. The milkman slides them into place, next to the other milk cans he's picked up at nearby farms, then jumps in the truck and drives off to the east, to the Ann Arbor Dairy.

Father and I head back up the driveway to the barn, now with me pushing the cart with the two empty milk cans in it, ready for the evening milking. My morning chores are over. I watch Father hitch our horses, Topsy and Buster, to the mower and head for the clover field.

Father planted that clover more than a year ago, in March of last year, walking in the field and working a hand cranked seeder. He cast the clover seeds on the ground between the stalks of wheat he'd planted

10

the previous fall. Last July he harvested the wheat, and by then the little clover shoots were coming up. He left the clover to grow all last summer and fall, and it bloomed out this spring. Now it's time to cut it. It will feed our cows, sheep and horses this coming winter.

The mower, a McCormick/Deering two wheeled machine, has a seat for Father to sit on above the axle, and a mechanism, powered by the wheels, that moves triangle shaped teeth back and forth above the cutting bar, leaving the hay in a nice swath behind the mower. Father says this modern farming implement is a great improvement over the use of a hand held scythe, dating back to Biblical times, which was the way my grandfather harvested clover and other crops in his youth. He still has that scythe, and I see him use it every once in awhile to mow small patches of weeds around the farm.

While Father is out in the clover field, mowing with the horses all morning, Marjorie, Lloyd and I play around the big elm tree by our house. After awhile, Mother gives each of us a small wicker basket and send us out to search for eggs our chickens have laid. The chickens have the run of the yard and lay their eggs in the coop, in the barn, and at various nooks and crannies in the yard. Sometimes we don't find a hiding spot until a chicken has laid eight or ten eggs in one place.

After we've collected the eggs, we carefully wipe them off and put them in egg cartons in our cool basement. There are plenty of eggs this morning and so Mother tells me to put out the "Eggs For Sale" sign down by the highway. People driving along the highway see the sign, stop and come up to the house to buy eggs. Funny thing, when we have lots of eggs and the sign says "twenty five cents a dozen," we sometimes have a hard time selling all of them. But when we don't have many eggs and our sign says "a dollar a dozen" we sell out right away.

At noontime Father returns from the mowing and I help him feed and water the horses before we go into the house to have our dinner. Mother has made potato soup with sausage chunks in it. It's delicious with her home baked bread.

After dinner, Father heads back to the clover field to finish the mowing. By the time he returns, it will be time for me to bring the cows in again for the evening milking.

11

Chapter Three

It is a few days later now. Yesterday Father raked the mowed clover, pulling our hay rake with Topsy and Buster, and today at dinner he tells us the hay is ready for bringing into the barn this afternoon. He asks if I would like to drive the horses while he and Uncle Herbert load the hay into the wagon. I can't believe my ears. It's the first time he's asked me to drive the horses.

As soon as dinner is over I hurry to the barn and watch Father hook the horses to the front of the wagon and attach the hay loader to the back. Our hay loader is a strange looking machine. It has a large drum-like cylinder, with spikes sticking out of it, that rolls along the ground. The cylinder scoops up the hay and throws it on a wide elevator device that brings it up and drops it onto the wagon rack where it can be forked into place.

Father, standing in the front, just behind the standards, drives the horses from the barn to the clover field while Uncle Herbert and I sit on the rack, dangling our legs over the side. When we pull through the gate into the field, Father stops the horses, hands me the reins and tells me to drive the horses down the neatly raked rows of hay. My job is to keep the horses going straight on either side of the rows so the hay loader can scoop up the hay into the wagon. Father and Uncle Herbert, working with pitchforks, will distribute it evenly.

Barely containing my excitement, I stand and guide the horses, sometimes tugging on the right hand rein and calling out "Gee," which the horses know means they should go to the right, or pulling on the left rein and calling out "Haw," when I want them to go to the left.

The first row of hay is near a fence row with brush, trees and high grass. A beautiful cock pheasant struts out of the grass and watches us go by. His bright feathers glisten in the afternoon sun for a minute before he disappears back in the tall grass.

Suddenly I hear Uncle Herbert cry, "Look out!" A big snake has just been brought up on the hay wagon by the hay loader. It's heading for the front of the wagon where Father and I are. Father and Uncle Herbert are standing on the hay, but I am standing on the front standard, two upright pieces of wood with several horizontal pieces of wood attached to them to keep the hay from going over the front of the wagon and onto the horses.

I look back to see Father trying to throw the snake off the wagon with the pitch fork. He misses, and the snake, a blue racer at least five feet long, slithers under my feet, off the wagon and onto the ground where he disappears into the grass. Even though it's a warm summer afternoon, I feel a chill and a shiver go up and down my back.

We are now approaching the north end of the field. We will soon have to make a turn to the right to follow the row of hay. Father decides that since there is a slight hill at the end of the field, right where we will turn, maybe he better drive the horses. If the horses turn too quickly, the wagon could tip and the hay would slide off onto the ground. Father takes the reins and I climb back, up on the hay, as we make the turn. Suddenly, I feel the wagon tip and the hay I'm standing on, starts sliding off the wagon rack. And me along with it!

The fall from the wagon feels like it's in slow motion. When I land on the ground there is some hay below me, cushioning my fall, and a lot more above me. I'm not hurt, but pretty scared.

I hear Father's muffled cries telling Uncle Herbert to stop using his pitch fork to move the hay off me because he might hit me with the tines. I struggle to get up as they clear away the hay with their hands and uncover me. They're overjoyed when they see that I'm not hurt. Father suggests I go rest in the shade of a nearby tree while they load the hay back up on the wagon. I gratefully accept his suggestion and watch them work. After awhile I lie back on the ground and look up at the white fluffy clouds moving across the bright blue sky.

Suddenly I hear Father's voice. "Raymond, the hay is back on the wagon. Would you like to drive the horses again?"

I must have dozed off, but this wakes me in a hurry. I scramble back on the wagon and stand on the front standard again. Father hands me the reins and says, laughing, "Raymond, maybe if I'd have let you drive before, this would not have happened." That makes me feel really good.

We go the rest of the way around the field with no more problems. When the wagon is full, I stand on the highest bar of the standards and the hay is piled up almost to my head. Uncle Herbert detaches the hay loader and Father takes the reins once more and we head for the barn. Tomorrow he'll unload the hay into the mow.

Grandpa is waiting for us at the barn when we return. He looks over the hay we brought in while I tell him excitedly about our adventure. When I'm done he says, "Seems to me you could use some fun after all that hard work. If you'll dig some worms in the morning, I'll take you fishing down at the creek tomorrow afternoon."

What a joy that will be!

Chapter Four

I wake excited. Fishing with Grandpa today! Immediately after chores and breakfast I head for the tool shed, find a shovel and begin to dig for worms.

I am digging near the big elm tree, pulling fat night crawlers from the ground and putting them in an empty coffee can I'd gotten from Mother, when suddenly I hear the sound of barking coming from our wood lot. I immediately think of our sheep.

Lambing time was a few months ago, back in late March and early April. Most of the ewes in our herd of sixty, had lambs. Father was up late many nights, checking on the ewes when they were about to give birth. Some had twins and so, by the end of April, we had about sixty new lambs cavorting in the barnyard. Marjorie, Lloyd and I loved waking up those mornings and running to see if there were any new lambs in the barn. We'd pick them up, carry them like babies and, as they got older, chase them around the barnyard. There isn't anything

Me with our newly shorn sheep in the back yard.

more fun to watch than young lambs running and jumping about on a nice spring day.

Even before the lambing, in early March, there was the sheep shearing. Father said it was easier for the baby lambs to suckle if the ewes didn't have as much wool on them. Also, if a ewe was having birthing problems, it would be much easier to help her if her wool was shorn.

It was a cold, but sunny Saturday March morning, when the Egler brothers, a couple of farmers in our neighborhood, came to shear our sheep.

We kept the sheep in the north end of our barn, the horses in the south end and the cows in the biggest section, in the middle. The Egler brothers set up their equipment in the sheep barn. They began by each spreading a heavy canvas cloth, about eight feet square, on the ground. That's where the sheep would be placed for shearing. Then they plugged in their electric sheep shears, wool clippers very similar to human hair clippers, only much larger.

Uncle Herbert came to help, and when the Egler brothers were ready, he and Father brought the sheep to them one by one. The brothers picked up each sheep, with their hind legs hanging down, and plunked them down on their rumps.

They held their heads under their arms and sheared them with the big clippers. The sheep were breathing in their faces all day, as if they were kissing them.

Most of the sheep didn't seem to mind the shearing. They didn't bleat much. Some of them kicked a bit at first, but then settled down. As soon as they were released though, they ran away and crowded in with the other sheep out in the barn yard, as far away from the shearers as they could get.

Marjorie, Lloyd and I watched the whole time, of course, but I also helped a bit. My job was to bring the wool, after it was shorn from the sheep, to the wool box.

The wool box we used has been in our family for a long time. Grandfather used it, and maybe his father before him. It was a wooden box with two sides, four feet long and sixteen inches wide, and each piece hinged to the bottom. Two more pieces, sixteen inches square, were also hinged to the bottom, sixteen inches apart. When the four sides were raised up, they formed a cube with every dimension sixteen inches. The sides, when folded up, were held together by two long hooks at each end. The box had grooves cut into the outside surfaces and we ran twine in those grooves to tie the wool.

After each sheep was shorn, I brought the wool to the wool box where it was sitting on a couple of stands. The cord to tie the wool was all in place across the bottom of the box as it lay open and flat. After the wool was stuffed into the box, and the sides brought up, Father would tie the cord, then remove the hooks on the sides, unfold the box flat on the stand, and there in the center was a nice cube of freshly shorn wool, each bale weighing eight to ten pounds.

The Egler brothers sheared all morning and then we stopped for dinner. Mother prepared a good noon meal for all of us; baked chicken, one of our own, with stuffing made from her home made bread. She also made mashed potatoes and gravy, a salad and apple pie, made from the last of the apples from last fall's crop. After dinner everybody talked for awhile and then we headed back to the barn to finish shearing the sheep.

By the middle of the afternoon the last of the sheep had been shorn. While the Egler brothers packed up their equipment, we finished tying up the last fleece. We had quite a pile of wool fleeces, tied in neat bundles, ready to take to the wool buyer.

After the sheep were sheared, they tended to stay in the barn more because it was still cold outside. "But," Father said, "They'll appreciate those short coats when it gets hot this summer."

A few weeks later Father and I herded the flock into the orchard for a few days, where they ate the grass, trimmed it better than any lawn mower. Then, three days ago we drove the whole flock out to the same wood lot and pasture field where the cows were grazing. After being confined to the barn yard all winter, they were very happy to be out there. The lambs born this spring were now mature enough to go to pasture with their mothers.

When we returned to the house after herding the sheep to the pasture lot, Father said that now we must not forget about them out there by themselves for the summer. Especially, we must listen for the sound of barking dogs. He said wild dogs can wreak havoc in a flock of sheep.

Now, at the sound of the barking, I whirl around, looking for my BB gun. The air rifle is a Christmas gift I received this past winter. Ever since then, I've been carrying it with me practically wherever I go. I spot it now, where I'd leaned it against the big old elm tree. I grab it, feeling very big and brave with the gun in my hands. Without telling my folks, I start running toward the wood lot, cutting across the corn field. The legs of my overalls are quickly soaked by the dew covering the corn. They feel heavy against my bare feet and legs as I run toward the sound of the barking.

Still feeling very brave, I approach the fence separating the wood lot from the cornfield. The barking is louder now. Suddenly, a little way into the wood lot, I see a big black hound dog attacking one of the sheep. The dog has the sheep trapped between two small trees and is biting and tearing at her viciously.

My bravery suddenly leaves me. I look down at my little air rifle and know it won't be of much use against that dog. I turn and sprint back to the house as fast as I can. I shout, "Dogs in the sheep," over and over, the whole way. Father comes out of the barn and I breathlessly tell him what I saw. He runs to the house, with me right on his heels, and tells Mother he'll get Grandpa's shot gun and go to the woods. When he runs out of the house with the double barrel twelve gauge a minute later, he shouts back over his shoulder that we are to stay there.

Mother and I sit on the front steps, Marjorie and Lloyd between us. I fondle my air rifle, she twists her apron strings nervously and tells us she's worried. Father has only one good eye, the left. The right one was severely damaged at birth and is of no use to him. Since he's right handed, shooting a gun, sighting it accurately, is not easy for him.

We wait, sitting together on the porch steps. I keep seeing frightening images of the big black dog and the sheep. I look over at Marjorie and Lloyd and see that they're worried too.

Suddenly we hear a tremendous boom echoing from the wood lot. Father has fired the gun. The report is so loud I'm sure he shot both barrels at once.

Did he shoot the dog? Is he in danger if he missed? Should we go to the wood lot? While we're trying to decide, we spot him walking past the old elm tree, coming toward the house.

We all hurry to meet him. "Are you all right?" Mother asks when we get close. "Yes," he says in a shaky voice. "There were two dogs. When I got there, one of them left the sheep it was attacking and came towards me, growling and showing his teeth. If I had missed him when I shot, I shudder to think what might have happened to me."

He sits on the steps and puts his head in his hands. We all sit silently with him.

A few moments later he raises his head and says to me, "The dog you saw, Raymond, the big black one, ran away after I shot the other one."

We sit quietly for a few more minutes and then he turns to me again and says, "There won't be any fishing today I'm afraid. I'm going to need your help rounding up the distraught and injured sheep and lambs and bringing them back to the barn. I'll call the vet to come and check on them."

He goes inside and places the call. Then he and I head back to the wood lot. When we get near the woods we start calling the sheep to come to us, but only a few respond. So, we walk into the woods, looking for them.

What we find is horrible. Sheep and lambs are lying here and there on the ground, either dead or in great pain from their injuries. We find some that are too badly injured and beyond our help. Father picks up a heavy tree limb. I watch when he swings it the first time, but then I turn away and don't watch any more.

21

We gather together the sheep that are all right, and those able to limp along, and head them towards the lane and up to the barn where the vet is already waiting for us.

After chores we have a quiet, somber supper. Marjorie and I don't have the heart to turn on the radio tonight.

"In the morning," Father says, "We will bury twenty sheep and lambs." There won't be fishing tomorrow either.

Chapter Five

It is a few days later now. The sad and scary memories of the sheep have faded a little and Grandpa renews his offer to go fishing.

After chores and breakfast, with my trusty air rifle in hand, I head back to the old elm tree to dig for worms again. The morning drifts by calmly and this time I finish with no interruption. When the coffee can is filled with angle worms, I head back to the house. I stop occasionally along the way, put down the can and take a shot at a pesky sparrow. There are many of them around the barn yard and in the fields. They roost all over the place, in the barn, the other farm buildings, and the haystacks. They eat a lot of seed and their droppings are a nuisance. My shots usually miss, but I keep trying.

When I get close to the house Mother calls out that dinner is ready. Mother's call is a high pitched "whoeee" that we can hear clear over to the barn. Father hears her there now and he comes too. We meet at the back door of the house and we both wash our hands at the new modern sink in the wash room. Then we head into the kitchen for dinner.

I gulp my food quickly, thinking all the time about the fishing trip. As soon as I'm done, I excuse myself and go back outside to wait for Grandpa. Grandma and Grandpa live just across the highway from us. I can see their house and garage from our front porch. I watch now as he opens his garage door, gets in his 1929 Model A Ford, and starts for our farm house.

He crosses the highway and the streetcar tracks at Parker Road and when he turns into our farm lane I run to meet him. He greets me cheerfully. He has two bamboo fishing poles, at least fifteen feet long, lying over the front seat and sticking out the back window, so I get in the back seat, behind him. And then we're on our way!

It's almost a mile from our farm house to Mill Creek. As we make our way along Parker Road, the dust rises in a huge plume behind us on the dirt road. Finally, we head down a hill and approach the old iron bridge spanning the creek. The bridge has a wooden plank decking that rattles loudly as we cross it. Once we're on the other side of the bridge, Grandpa pulls off to the side of the road and parks the car.

This is our favorite fishing hole. I jump out of the car, carrying my can of worms, and head down the well worn path in my bare feet to find just the right spot for our fishing. Grandpa follows, carrying the fishing poles.

"You chose a good spot, Raymond," he says when he catches up to me. He puts hooks and worms on the lines and hands me a pole. I raise the pole and, using the strong overhead motion Grandpa has taught me, send the line and hook and worm out into the creek. Grandpa has also put bobbers, cork stoppers from gallon jugs of cider and vinegar, on each line. The bobbers, floating on the surface of the water, will let us know when a fish is caught on the hook underwater.

We sit on the grassy bank and wait for the bobbers to tell us a fish has found our worms. I swish my bare feet around in the water at the edge of the creek and look around. Across the creek a huge willow tree with long drooping limbs covered with slender leaves, is shading us from the hot summer sun. To our left, a loud croaking sound comes from beneath an elderberry bush. A big bullfrog, resting on a large stone sticking out of the water, is sending out his happy message. The elderberry bush is in full bloom, its slim branches full of delicate white blossoms. No wonder that frog is enjoying himself.

24

I lie back on the grassy bank and watch two turkey buzzards sailing aimlessly among a few white clouds in the beautiful blue sky. I'm sure they're the same two I saw above our fields few weeks ago.

"Your bobber is moving upstream. You better tend to your pole," Grandpa says, interrupting my reverie. I sit up quickly and, sure enough, the bobber is moving. I grab my pole and yank upward as hard as I can, hoping to set the hook in the fish. The pole bends into a U, the tip almost reaching the water. Suddenly, the fish comes flying out of the creek and lands with a thud at my feet on the bank. I quickly lay the pole on the ground, grab the still flapping fish, and carry it farther away from the water. I don't want it to escape.

I am really happy with my catch. Grandpa takes the hook from the fish's mouth. I've caught a sucker, a bottom feeder. The fish measures almost sixteen inches. Its mouth is shaped like a suction cup, so he can swim lazily along the sandy bottom of the creek and suck up anything that is edible, including the worm on my line.

Grandpa starts putting another worm on my hook when he notices that the bobber on his pole is moving upstream. Leaving me to finish the job, he grabs his pole and quickly brings his fish, which is struggling very hard, to the creek bank. His fish, also a sucker, is even longer than mine.

Grandpa has brought along a large bucket in which to put any fish we might catch. Now he fills the bucket from the creek and puts in the fish, to keep them in good shape till we get home. We settle back once again, sitting on the creek bank, poles in hand, waiting patiently for more fish.

There are rock bass in this creek. They're pan fish, like blue gills, but they grow to a pretty fair size. They hang out around rocks or tree stumps in the water. They're not bottom feeders. We've seen them jump out of the water and grab a low flying mosquito, or an insect along the shore. They like worms too. They grab them if they wash in from the shore. But, they're not biting today. Nor is anything else. So, after about another hour sitting on the creek bank, Grandpa says maybe it's time to head for home.

*My paternal grandparents, Jacob and
Elizabeth "Betta" Schairer*

"I'll clean our catch, Grandma will make some fried fish patties, and you can stay for supper. What do you say?" What could I say!

We load the poles and the fish in the car and head back to Grandpa's house. I put away the tackle and the fishing poles while Grandpa cleans the fish. Suckers have lots of bones. Not only the usual backbone and rib bones like the rock bass, but they are also full of little bones all through their bodies. But Grandpa has a system. After he takes out the ribs and backbone, he grinds the rest of the fish in a hand cranked meat grinder. This way the bones are no problem. Then Grandma makes huge fish patties, covers them with bread crumbs and fries them in butter—made from the cream of our cow's milk. When she takes them from the frying pan, crisp and golden brown, they look beautiful. She picks out a loaf of her home made bread from the bread box on the counter, cuts thick slices, and slathers on more of that butter. She adds a thick layer of honey from the bees Uncle Herbert raises on his farm. To top off the meal, she pours me a glass of milk, also from our cows, and gives me a huge homemade sugar cookie for dessert. By the time I finish, all sad thoughts about our sheep and the dogs are far from my mind.

The clock on Grandma's kitchen shelf says it's once again time for me to help Father cool the evening milk. Grandpa walks me to the highway and watches for traffic as I scoot across. While stirring the milk I tell Father about our fishing and, when we're done, we go in the house and I tell the stories again to Mother, Marjorie and Lloyd.

Chapter Six

It is now a few days after the Fourth of July. Time to harvest the wheat crop. At breakfast this morning, Father announces he will start cutting the wheat today. The twelve acre field of wheat, larger than most in our neighborhood, is along the west side of Parker Road, halfway between our farm house and Mill Creek, where we'd gone fishing.

After morning chores, Father harnesses the horses, three this time, and hooks them to the grain binder. The grain binder has a cutter similar to the hay mower but this machine also gathers the cut stalks of wheat into bundles. After the wheat stalks are cut by the mower part, all the heads facing the same way, they fall onto a four foot wide canvas conveyor belt which carries them to a device that collects and ties them into bundles with twine made of Jute. Then the bundles of wheat drop to the ground and end up in rows across the field. It looks like a picture in a magazine.

Father climbs onto the grain binder's seat and starts the horses down our farm lane. There isn't a safe place for me to ride on the machine, so I follow in my bare feet, as usual. Walking along Parker Road, a gravel road, is pretty uncomfortable on my feet, but I'm excited thinking about what is ahead.

When we get to the field of wheat, I run ahead and open the gate. On the right, near the entrance to the field, is a beautiful large hickory nut tree that Grandfather planted years ago, along with many of the other trees on our farm. In the fall it has the largest hickory nuts I've ever seen.

I follow along behind the grain binder, watching the bundles of wheat drop to the ground. I spot a couple of monarch butterflies flitting about along the fence row. I turn to watch them till they are out of sight.

Ouch! I'm not looking where I'm going. I've stepped on the stem of a Canadian thistle. The prickly little thorns pierce the bottom of my right foot. I sit down and pick out the thistles, while the binder continues on its way. Then I jump up, limping a little on my sore foot, and run after the grain binder. By the time I catch up to it, Father has gone almost all the way around the field for the first time. I decide it's too hot to follow him anymore. When we pass the gate where we came into the field I stop by the giant hickory tree.

I sit in the shade, with my back to the tree, and watch Father continue across the field, leaving nice rows of wheat bundles behind him. I look up into the branches and spot a squirrel looking down out of a hole high in the tree. He is watching me as carefully as I am watching him. In a few minutes his head disappears back into the hole and I turn away to watch the few white clouds in the bright blue sky, drifting along in an easterly direction. The sun is making it pretty warm even in the shade.

Suddenly, I hear Mother calling my name. I must have dozed off. I rub my eyes and come awake and she asks how everything is coming along with the wheat cutting. She has brought a jug of water for Father and me. I ask her to sit in the shade with me and we wait for Father to come around the field. I ask her where my brother and sister are. "With Grandma and Grandpa," she says.

When Father comes around to where we are sitting, he stops the horses, climbs off the binder and comes over and joins us. He is happy to have a drink of water and thanks Mother for bringing it. The horses are happy for the rest and put their heads down and nibble off a few mouthfuls of grass. Eating the plump grass takes away their thirst.

After about fifteen minutes Father climbs back on the grain binder and gets back to cutting the field of wheat. I walk back slowly to the house with Mother. It's too warm to hurry.

When we get back to the house Mother starts getting supper ready and I head for the barn yard to get the cows from the pasture field for the evening milking. By the time I get back to the barn with the cows Father has returned from the wheat field. He unhooks the horses from the binder, takes off their harnesses and puts them in the barn yard. They drink from the same big tank as the cows and we head to the house for supper. Afterward we'll go back to the barn to milk the cows and cool the milk.

The next morning, after chores and breakfast, Father calls Uncle Herbert to see if he can come and help set up the wheat bundles laying in the field from yesterday's cutting. When Uncle Herbert arrives, we get into his old car and ride down the road to the field. It is quite a sight to see the whole field of wheat bundles laying on the ground in those straight rows.

Then they go to work. I watch as they each pick up two bundles of wheat, one under each arm and set them up, with the heads of the wheat at the top, and the bottom ends of the wheat stalks planted firmly on the ground. They place the bundles close to each other and when they have eight pairs set up, they form a "shock." They line the wheat shocks in north south running rows so the sun can shine on both sides of the shocks during the day. This helps in the drying process, especially if it rains.

They set up shocks of wheat all morning. I try helping at first, dragging a few bundles to them, but they're too heavy for me, so I sit under the hickory tree again and watch them work until lunch time. Then we drive back to the house and eat the nice lunch Mother prepared for us; sandwiches, fruit from the orchard, and lemonade.

After lunch, Father and Uncle Herbert go back to finish shocking the wheat. I stay behind and play with Marjorie until it's time for me to get the cows from the pasture. Just before I leave, Father and Uncle Herbert return from the field, their task complete. Father says, "It's a beautiful sight, all those shocks of wheat standing in the field." Then he adds, "Next week we'll haul the wheat to the barn and you can drive the horses again."

I remember watching them do this last year. They went across the field along each row of shocks, and Uncle Herbert pitched the bundles from each shock to Father on the wagon. Father placed the bundles in neat layers across the wagon rack until he had ten or twelve layers on the wagon. Then he drove the horses to the barn and unloaded the wheat on the upper floor of the barn. He put the bundles at the opposite end of the barn from the hay mow. We will do that again this year. That is where the threshing machine will stand in a few weeks, when the time comes to separate the grain from the bundles of wheat. That's always an exciting time.

Chapter Seven

We have a few cats on the farm, in and around the barn. They love the fresh milk we give them, directly from the cows at milking time, but they're not really pets. We don't have a dog, though the other day I overheard Father tell Mother that maybe we

Me, Lloyd and Marjorie with our dog.

ought to have a dog around to prove to me that all dogs are not like the ones that attacked the sheep.

But, I do have some pets. Earlier in the year, at Easter time, Grandma and Grandpa gave me a gift of a pair of little ducklings. I have never had anything like them before. When I first got them, they were so little, like tiny balls of fuzzy fur. I was delighted and Marjorie was too.

Mother worried though. Where will we keep them? The weather outside at that time of year can sometimes still be harsh. "How about in the basement, near the new furnace?" I asked.

"A good idea," she said. So, with Father helping, we made a big box-like pen for them to eat, sleep and play around in. We put the box near the furnace. Marjorie and I fed them a couple of times a day, very faithfully, bits of bread and oatmeal until they were old enough to eat wheat and corn. They grew fast as the weeks went by. We put a large basin of water in the pen with them and they climbed in and swam around and drank all the water they wanted.

They continued to grow, developing beautiful white feathers all over their bodies. They were big enough now to jump over the sides of the pen and romp all around the basement. They were kind of messy at times and got into things they shouldn't. They tried Mother's patience to the point that finally one day she announced we would have to find another place for those pesky ducks.

"Where will they go?" I asked. Then it occurred to me, several weeks had gone by and the weather had warmed to the point where our not so little ducks could now do very well outside the house. "How about the woodshed?" I asked. "Perfect," said Father. Most of the wood stored there had already been burned in the furnace during the winter, so there was plenty of room for the ducks. And they would have easy access to the yard around the house.

They continued to grow. They would strut around in the back yard, searching for bugs of all kinds to eat. They especially liked flies. They would jump into the air trying to catch them. Marjorie and I would sit on the step leading into the woodshed and those two ducks would climb on our laps. They'd put their long white feathered necks and heads with those bright black eyes and yellow beaks around our necks and sort of give us a little hug. We loved those ducks!

One day, as they followed me to the windmill to pump water to cool the milk, I heard a loud quacking sound coming from the smaller one. It turned out she was a female and the other one was a male. His quacking stayed very soft. There was now quite a distinction between the two. That female really let us know when she was around.

Every day I pumped water and ran back and forth between the well and the well house to cool the milk. Sometimes the ducks would follow me, sometimes not. Today, on my last trip back to the well house, they didn't follow me and I lost track of where they were as I went to the barn to see what Father was doing.

Then, a little later, we went in for dinner. I was not concerned about the ducks. But, after dinner, when I came back out and remembered I hadn't seen them or heard them for quite some time, I began to worry about where they might be.

I looked all over. I started at the woodshed. Maybe they are taking a little nap in the shade of the building.

Not there.

I searched around the well house. Then over to the windmill, where I last remembered seeing them. Still no ducks. I go back to the house, almost in tears, and tell Mother I can't find my ducks.

She joins me in the search. We go out back to the big old elm tree, where there is lots of shade. Still no ducks. Now everyone is concerned, including Father, when we fill him in. The ducks have disappeared.

We all sit on the back porch steps, Lloyd in Mother's lap, Marjorie between Father and me. We are sad. Marjorie and I can't hold back some tears. Father finally says, "I think what probably happened is that the ducks found the open driveway that crosses the streetcar tracks onto the highway. And since they would make friends with anyone, someone traveling along the highway saw them, stopped and picked them up. I don't think we will ever see them again."

In response, Marjorie and I shed a few more tears. But, then Mother says that she had a phone call, over our new phone system, from her mother, my Grandma Hinderer, who lives in Chelsea, about eight miles west of our farm. She has invited us all to come to her house tomorrow, Sunday, after church, for dinner and a visit with her. She lives alone. Her husband, my other Grandpa, died a short while before I was born.

This cheers us up a little and now it is once again time to get the cows from the pasture field. The walk in the dusty path will, I am sure, soothe my aching heart.

33

Chapter Eight

Sunday morning breaks forth, looking like a beautiful, warm, sunny day. After the usual morning chores are done, (the wind is blowing today, so I don't have to pump water, only stir the milk to cool it,) it's time for breakfast and then a bath.

We're going to church this morning. So, I will wear shoes today, Oxford type, with knee length, rather heavy socks. I'll also wear knickerbockers, pants Mother made for me from hand-me-downs furnished by my cousin Roger who is a bit older and taller than I am. The knickerbockers' legs come just below my knees and an elastic fastening makes them puff out slightly just above my knees. A nice clean white shirt and little black bow tie complete my attire. I am presentable, but quite uncomfortable, to say the least.

Marjorie is dressed in a nice, colorful, figured dress that Mother made out of cow feed bags she bought at the feed store, a familiar custom in those

Marjorie, Lloyd and me, probably on a Sunday. Note the shoes. That's Grandpa Jacob in the background with his Model T Ford.

Me, my mother and father, and Marjorie. Our 1926 Ford is in the background.

days. Lloyd is dressed just like me, wearing one of my old knicker-bockers that Mother has altered to fit him. Mother is wearing a dress she sewed herself, but Father has on a real store-bought suit consisting of pants, vest and suit coat over a white shirt and tie.

Dressed in our best, we head out of the house toward the shed and our 1926 Ford sedan. We all get in, except for Father, who has to hand crank the engine to start it. I get the front seat next to Father. Mother, Marjorie and Lloyd get in the back seat. A few turns of the crank and the engine starts. Father gets in the driver's seat and we are on our way out of the shed, down the driveway, toward the streetcar tracks and the highway that will take us to Chelsea and church.

But, something happens. As Father turns out of our driveway to cross the streetcar tracks, the engine coughs and dies and the front end of the car comes to rest on the tracks. Wearing a concerned expression, Father gets out of the car and cranks the engine. Nothing happens. Again he tries and still the engine won't start.

He begins to get warm with the effort of the cranking. Taking off his suit coat he tries cranking again. Still nothing. Suddenly we all hear the clanging of the streetcar coming along the tracks, past our barn and windmill. Panic sets in. Father starts pushing the car back off the tracks. I open the passenger door and stand on the wide running board, craning over the top of the car, looking for the street car. Father sees it before me, instantly decides he can't get the car off the tracks in time, and yells to us to get out of the car. I jump off the running board, farther than I ever jumped before, or since, and end up well away from the car.

Father rushes around the side of the car to help Mother, Marjorie and Lloyd. Too late. Mother is too petrified to do anything other than hug my sister and brother as the streetcar, with its big bumper, called a cow catcher, hits the front end of our car with a big crunching crash, and shoves it off the tracks as it goes by. Father yanks open the back door and looks in to find the rest of our family unhurt, but terribly shook up. Marjorie and Lloyd are crying hard.

By this time the conductor of the streetcar has stopped his machine and is running back toward us. He says to Father breathlessly, "I saw you trying to push the car off the track and thought you were going to make it, so I didn't start to stop until it was too late." After assuring himself that we were not hurt, he excused himself, saying he had to get back to the streetcar to keep on schedule. The streetcar began moving again and left us standing beside the track, thinking about what to do.

Father helps Mother, Marjorie and Lloyd out of the car and we all start walking slowly back to the house. Once inside, we all sit in the living room, trying to collect our wits and rest a bit. All but Father. After changing his clothes, he goes to the barn and harnesses the horses. He finds a short chain and leads the team back to the wrecked car next to the tracks. I watch from the porch as he hooks the chain to the back bumper of the car and, guiding the horses, tows it back to the shed.

It sits there, a sad looking mess!

After putting the horses back in the barn, Father returns to the house to help figure out what we will do next.

Mother calls her mom, to tell her what has happened and that we won't make it to church and her house today. A disappointment to everyone! But, Grandma tells Mother not to worry. She will call my two uncles, Mother's brothers, who own a grocery store in town, and ask them put together a pot luck dinner. Then she and both their families will drive out to our farm and we will have a get-together to help us forget our upsetting experience of the morning.

This sounds like a great idea and Mother agrees enthusiastically. After she hangs up the phone, she suggests we kids take a nap while she and Father set the table, bring in extra chairs and get ready for the company. Marjorie, Lloyd and I head upstairs, but we're too excited by the events of the morning, and the upcoming visit, to be able to sleep.

About two o'clock we hear our relatives drive up the driveway to the house. It takes two cars to get them all here, Grandma Hinderer and two sets of aunts and uncles, Mildred and Otto and Matilda and Wilbur Hinderer, plus our young cousins.

We have a good time eating, visiting and playing in the big yard by the house. The adults talk over the morning's experience, and try to help my folks figure out what to do next. And soon the afternoon is gone and it is time once again to do the evening chores. Our relatives climb into their cars and drive back to their homes in Chelsea.

Father and I change into our working clothes. I take off my Sunday shoes and I am, happily, barefoot again. I run to the barn, through the barnyard gate, down the lane, calling the cows. It's a little later than usual and they are already coming along the lane towards the barn. I wait for them to pass by me and then follow them, soothing my bare feet in that wonderful dusty path. When the cows are all back in the barn,

Me, Lloyd and Marjorie, dressed in our Sunday best.

Father milks them and we take the milk to the well house. I stir, while the windmill pumps the cool water. Then, it's back to the house. I am one tired boy.

It has been quite a day. I head up to bed early and fall asleep wondering what tomorrow might bring for me and our family.

38

Chapter Nine

Father has been busy these last few days, trying to find a new car to replace the old Ford wrecked in Sunday's accident. Mother has been canning summer fruits and vegetables for next winter. I just play with Marjorie in the yard. We still both miss those ducks.

Late this afternoon, Uncle Herbert comes by to let Father know that the threshing machine will be coming into the neighborhood in a few days and we will be the first stop. We have been waiting for this day since we brought the wheat into the barn a few weeks ago. I got to drive the horses again, as I did when we brought in the hay. We went across the field, along each row of shocks, and Uncle Herbert pitched the bundles from each shock to Father on the wagon. Father placed the bundles in neat layers across the wagon rack until he had ten or twelve layers. Then we headed back to the barn and unloaded the bundles on the upper floor of the barn, at the opposite end from the hay mow where the horses and wagon stand.

Tonight Father gets a call from Mr. Horning, the owner of the threshing machine. He says he will be bringing the thresher to our farm late tomorrow afternoon to set it up for the following day.

The next morning, after chores are done, we sweep out the barn and the granary bins to get them ready for the thresher and for the threshed wheat. Mother bustles around the house getting ready to feed the five or six men, mostly neighbor farmers, who will be coming to help us thresh.

All day I wait with great anticipation for the moment I will see the big tractor, pulling the threshing machine, come along Parker Road from the south, past Uncle Herbert's farm, to ours. It's late in the afternoon, I am sitting on the front porch, when I suddenly spot it. The tractor is moving very slowly, about two miles per hour, so it will be awhile before it will be heading up our driveway to the barn.

The tractor is a huge machine. It has a steam engine like the locomotive trains, with a furnace to heat water and make steam to run the engine. The furnace has to be periodically stoked with chunks of wood. The wheels are enormous. The front two are at least three feet high, and the back ones more than six feet tall and two feet wide. They're all made of iron and when they roll along the gravel road, the little stones make a loud crunching sound as they are crushed by the wheels of the heavy machine. I know I'll never forget that sound.

The threshing machine is a long box, with many belts and pulleys adorning the sides. On one end is a platform where the thresher man will stand and feed the bundles of wheat into an opening in the machine. At the other end is a long pipe where the straw stalks and chaff will blow out to make a huge straw stack in the barn yard.

The tractor comes slowly up the lane from Parker Road, turns into our yard and stops in front of the barn. Mr. Horning gets off the tractor and unhooks the threshing machine. Then he climbs back on the tractor and turns it around so he'll be able to hook its front end to the threshing machine and push it into the barn. First though, he turns the long straw pipe on top of the thresher, so it is pointing straight out the door on the other side of the barn, to the barnyard, where the straw will be stacked.

Once he pushes the thresher into the barn, Mr. Horning backs the tractor away, just far enough so he can attach a long belt, made of leather and cloth, about ten inches wide, nearly half an inch thick, and some fifty feet long, onto the tractor drive pulley and then onto a big pulley on the side of the threshing machine. Then he moves the tractor a little, so there is proper tension on the belt. Finally he pushes a lever on the tractor and the pulleys both turn, the power supplied by the tractor, and the thresher is ready to do its work. He turns off the tractor and puts chucks under the wheels so it can't move out of position.

One more thing to do. He fits a smaller pipe on the side of the thresher and points it into the granary where the wheat will go. "We are ready for threshing tomorrow morning," he tells Father. A car drives into our yard just then. It's someone come to give Mr. Horning a ride home.

Next morning we finish the chores early, just as Mr. Horning arrives and fires up the wood burner in the tractor to heat the water for the steam needed to run the engine. About an hour later Uncle Herbert and three other farm neighbors drive into the yard. They've come to help with the threshing.

Father warns me to stay out of the way so I won't get hurt. I find a place near the haymow and, sitting on an old box, watch the men as they put the wheat bundles on the thresher's platform. There Mr. Horning first cuts the twine holding the bundles together. Then, working with a small hook, he spreads out the bundles and feeds them, heads first, into the opening on the thresher. The bundles disappear into the dark insides of the huge machine and are magically transformed. The grains of wheat are knocked out of the heads of the stalks and come shooting out in a golden spray from the metal tube that points into the granary, while the straw and chaff are blown out the big long metal tube and into the barnyard.

Time goes fast and at twelve thirty it's time to stop for dinner. Everybody heads for the house to clean up a bit. There's a bench out in the yard with several basins of water and a couple of bars of soap. The men wash the dust and dirt from their arms and faces, then dry themselves with towels hanging on a nearby rack. Then we head into the dining room, to eat a delicious meal of roast beef, potatoes and gravy, sweet corn, Jell-O salad, apple pie for dessert, and tea or coffee. Mother and all the farmers' wives always try to outdo each other preparing these threshing dinners, and the men enjoy them all.

41

Then back to work. By late afternoon the threshing is done. The wheat bins are full and a huge straw stack stands in the barn yard, expertly built by two men who laid the straw out properly as it came out from the machine.

The men leave quickly. They also have evening chores to do when they get home. Mr. Horning disconnects the big drive belt from the tractor and threshing machine, turns the tractor around, hooks it back up to the threshing machine and pulls it from the barn to begin the journey down the road to the next farm.

I watch that big tractor and threshing machine going slowly down the road until they are out of sight.

Chapter Ten

After the threshers leave, I head down the dusty lane to bring our cows in for milking. When we get back and the cows see the huge new straw stack in the barn yard, they run over to it, poke their big heads into the nice soft straw to brush the flies from their faces. Then they rub their furry sides against the straw—for the same reason. It takes Father and me quite awhile to get them away from the straw stack and into the barn for milking. When we are done with the milking they can't wait to get back out of the barn, to lay on the soft straw around the bottom of the stack. Father says they are the "proverbial contented cows" tonight.

The cows are not the only ones happy with the new straw stack. The many sparrows that roost in every farm building, making nests in every nook and cranny they can find, are also drawn to the straw stack. In the next few days they come in huge numbers to make their nests in it. They do the same at other nearby farms too.

Now it's the first Sunday evening since the threshing day. As Father and I head up to the house after milking the cows and cooling the milk, a couple of cars turn off the highway and come up the driveway. We don't recognize them. When they stop, Father goes to greet them. I stay behind as the driver of the first car gets out to talk to Father, but I can hear the conversation from where I am standing. The man has a strong Italian accent and he is asking Father whether he and his friends could capture some of the sparrows that are roosting in our straw stack.

"What would you want with the sparrows?" Father asks.

The man replies that he and his friends are from Detroit and that the Great Depression has been hard on them financially. They are looking for some meat to add to their meals. I can't believe my ears!

Father asks him with some surprise in his voice, "How can you get enough meat from a sparrow to be of any use?"

"Well," the man tells Father, "After skinning the feathers off the little birds, we cut off only the breast meat and, if we have enough birds, our wives can make a big pasta dish with the meat. It will help our families from going hungry."

I still can't believe what I am hearing, but Father says they can try their luck at catching the sparrows.

At this, the men all get out of their cars and we see that they have several long poles sticking out the back windows, just like the fishing poles that poked out of my Grandpa's car when we went fishing. The men pull the poles from the cars, and I see that they have what looks like fish netting attached to them.

Father leads them along the driveway to the barnyard. I follow behind. It's almost dark now as we enter the barnyard. The cows laying around the straw stack get up from their comfortable positions on the new straw and move to the fence, as far away from us as they can get. They look at us, curious as I am, to see what will happen.

With two men holding each pole, they unfurl the netting between them, to make a big net, about ten feet high and ten feet long. Then, in two groups of four men each, holding the poles and netting upright, they carefully approach one side of the straw stack so as not to disturb the unsuspecting sparrows in their nests. With the two nets extended, they cover almost twenty feet of the straw stack. After they all get into position, the men simultaneously slap the side of the straw stack with the poles and nets, and the sparrows, rudely awakened from their sleep, fly out of their nests and are caught in the net.

The men quickly close the net poles together so the sparrows are tangled in the netting. They then take them back to the cars and, one by one, get them out of the netting and put them into a large cage in the back seat of one of the cars. A few sparrows escape during this process, but the men manage to get most of them into the cage.

Then they repeat the same thing on the other side of the straw stack. When the cages are full of twittering sparrows, the men get into their cars and, thanking Father profusely, head out our driveway, turn onto the highway and are gone.

When we leave the barnyard the cows quickly go back to lay down around the straw stack.

Father and I go back to the house and, over supper, we tell Mother, Marjorie and Lloyd the story of the sparrow catchers.

Chapter Eleven

The next morning, after the usual morning chores, we have breakfast and get ready to go to town. How will we get there? We have no car anymore. We'll ride the streetcar, of course—the reason we have no car. It's scheduled to pass by our farm at ten o'clock—the same time it hit our car on that Sunday morning a couple of weeks ago.

We walk down to the end of our driveway and stand, looking down the streetcar tracks to the east. With bell clanging, here she comes! Father waves his white handkerchief high over his head. This time the conductor sees him and stops the streetcar at the end of our driveway to pick us up.

We all clamber aboard and are on our way. The streetcar is a rickety old machine, but the seats are fairly comfortable. We all look out the windows and watch as we pass the many neighboring farms. After a few miles we come to a little village called Lima Center, which has three or four houses, a country store and a streetcar depot.

After a brief stop we continue into Chelsea, passing through a large peat marsh. Then on to the depot. We get off there and walk to Grandma Hinderer's house nearby.

She greets us warmly, and has a simple lunch prepared for us. We eat heartily, and quickly, and then Marjorie and Lloyd stay with Grandma while Mother, Father and I walk uptown to do our shopping. Father heads off to the Harper Pontiac car dealer on West Middle Street

Grandma Hinderer.

to look at cars, while Mother and I walk to the Streiter Brothers store on Main Street to buy me some new school clothes. She picks out a pair of bib overalls, a blue chambray shirt, some knee high socks and a pair of new shoes. My feet have grown some during the summer barefoot season. These new shoes are something else. All leather, with high tops that came up almost to my knees, and sporting a side pocket for a big Boy Scout knife. Imagine that!

Then we walk along Main Street to Hinderer Brothers, my uncles' grocery store and meat market. While Mother visits with Uncle Otto and Uncle Wilbur, I wander about the store. I see a big round of cheese on a counter. A cheese cutting knife is next to it, so I cut off a sizable piece. Nearby is a barrel filled with crackers. I grab a few of them and munch away as I continue to the back of the store where the big meat cooler is. The meat is kept cold with large cakes of ice, taken from the local lakes late in the winter and stored in ice houses.

It's nice and cool in there, and I continue eating my cheese and crackers while I survey the big pieces of uncooked beef, pork and chickens hanging by their feet from racks overhead. Customers come into the cooler, pick out what they want, and Uncle Wilbur gets it down for them. I stay in the cooler for some time, enjoying the cool air, a nice relief from the August heat, before Mother finds me, saying it's time to go back to Grandma's house. I say goodbye to my uncles and we go back to Grandma's house to wait for Father.

We don't wait long before we hear the honking of a car horn in front of the house. Father has bought a new car, a General Motors Pontiac. We all rush out of the house, down the wooden porch steps, to where he has parked it in the driveway.

What a beautiful sight! Our first new car! We all climb into it, try out the cushioned seats, blow the horn, and breathe in that new car smell, something we have never had the chance to enjoy before. We are all very excited.

Father calms us after a bit, reminding us it's time to head for home to do the evening chores. We say goodbye to Grandma Hinderer, and Father backs the car out onto the street and heads us towards the farm. It is a much more comfortable ride than the one we had into town on the streetcar. When we arrive home, Father turns into the driveway and stops near the shed where the car will be parked. We all get out and after one last long look at our new car, head for the house to change our clothes. Then, it's time once again for me to walk the dusty lane and get the cows from pasture.

Chapter Twelve

It's Labor Day weekend, the last weekend before the Country School opens for another nine month session. Every year at this time, some of the families whose children attend the school gather to help get everything ready. The men mow the grass, cut the weeds that have grown during the summer, and rake the school yard so it looks nice.

While the men are doing these tasks, the women wash the windows, sweep the floor and dust all the desks we will be sitting in next week. The outside toilets, two separate little buildings, one for the boys and one for the girls, also get spruced up. The woodshed, which stands between the two toilets, is filled with the firewood supply for the winter. There is a well in the school yard, with a hand pump just like the one under our windmill. That is checked too. (With all my experience, who do you think gets to pump all the water for our school's needs?)

The Country School. It still looks very much like this today, though it has been a private residence for decades.

Some of the fathers put up a swing, two ropes and a wooden seat tied to the limb of a big maple tree just northwest of the schoolhouse. There is also a brand new, hand pumped merry-go-round this year. There is of course a baseball field, complete with a pitcher's mound. And, all of this is surrounded by many tall maple trees. They will soon be getting their beautiful fall colors.

Everyone takes a last look around. The schoolhouse is ready for the school bell, hanging just outside the front door, to call us to classes next week, the day after Labor Day.

The weekend passes quickly. We drive to church on Sunday. Riding in the new car is still a thrill. After church, Mother prepares a special Sunday dinner for us, and then Marjorie and I play around in the front yard until it is time for me to get those cows to the barn again for the evening milking.

Labor Day dawns bright the next morning. When the morning chores are done I ask Father if we could go for another ride in the new car. "Good idea," he says, "And maybe we can talk your mother into making us a picnic lunch and we can stop and eat along the way." That's exactly what we do. We drive around the countryside in the sunny morning, looking to see what our farm neighbors have been doing this summer.

At one point in our touring, I suddenly realize we are by the creek where Grandpa and I have gone fishing. "Let's stop here to eat our lunch," I suggest. Mother and Father agree and we stop and unpack. After the meal, we sit on the creek bank, watching the water silently slipping by, the big willow tree shading us as it did when I was here fishing earlier in the summer.

The afternoon is about over when we pack up to leave. The never-ending farm chores still lie ahead of us, and plans must be made for tomorrow, the first day of school.

Tuesday morning I get to sleep in a little later. During the school year I don't have morning chores to do, except on the weekends. However, I still help after school. The minute I wake I remember, "This is it, first day of fifth grade."

Breakfast is a big bowl of wheat, right from our barn, which Mother has cooked on the wood stove for twenty four hours, so the grains will be tender. It's very chewy, but tasty. Marjorie eats with me because this year she will start going to school too.

We get dressed in our new clothes, Marjorie in the nice dress Mother made, me in the clothes we bought on our trip to town last week. I am especially proud of my new high top shoes with the knife pocket attached!

Mother fixes us a lunch of fried sandwiches with peanut butter and honey, a fresh carrot from the garden and a big red apple. She gives us a quick kiss and we leave the house and hurry along the driveway to Parker Road. We carefully cross the streetcar tracks and the highway and head for the school across the way.

The schoolyard is already full of children and parents greeting friends and classmates they've not seen all summer. Everybody seems to have arrived at the same time. There are twenty five students, from five years old to fifteen. This will make up the grades from one through eight. Our teacher, Mrs. Steinbach, is there at the doorway and beckons us to come in. When we are all inside, the few parents who came with their young children, leave to go back to their homes.

Mrs. Steinbach directs us to our designated seats for the start of the new season. Our desks have wrought iron ends and hardwood tops, seats and backs. The tops have a place hollowed out for pens and pencils and an ink well between the pen and pencil holders. The ink wells, filled with ink, are a great temptation for us boys. If a girl with nice long hair sits ahead of us, we have been known to dip the ends of her hair into our ink wells. And, of course, Mrs. Steinbach has been known to quickly put an end to this sort of nonsense with a sharp slap of a ruler on the offending hand!

My seat is next to the big wood stove—a great location during the winter months. In the cold season I start the fire early in the mornings, so the school is warm when we start. Mrs. Steinbach's desk is at the south end of the building, facing us students. This is a little confusing because I, along with the rest of the students, sit facing south, but the maps in our geography books indicate that we are looking north.

The morning goes quickly. I am so excited to be here, I can hardly pay attention to anything Mrs. Steinbach is saying or trying to teach us. When it's time for lunch, Marjorie joins a few of her young friends to eat her sandwich, while I gather together with two of my classmates to eat mine. When we want something to drink, we go to the back of the room, where a stoneware crock with a spigot at the bottom sits on a table. There is a metal cup, hanging from a hook nearby. Everybody uses the same cup.

My schoolmates, Fred Covert, Phil Smith, Horace Maichele, and me.

My friends and I have all come to school with the same high top shoes with the knife pockets in them. And we all have knives. After we eat, someone suggests, "Let's play Mumble de Pegs." This is a new game for me so I ask, "How do we do that?" We all go outside.

Like all Boy Scout knives, ours have a long blade and a short one. My friends demonstrate how you extend the short blade all the way out and then open the long blade part way, so it forms a right angle to the handle. Since both blades emerge from the same side, the knife now looks like a letter T, with the handle and short blade forming the top, and the long blade forming the stem. Then you stick the long blade about an inch into the ground and, with the end of your middle finger, you flick up quickly on the end of the handle. If everything works right, the long blade pulls out of the ground, the knife flips into the air and sticks into the ground—blades first! Not easy to do, I find.

54

While we are trying to master this, the girls are playing "Auntie-I-Over." They form two groups, one on each side of the schoolhouse, and throw a tennis ball over the roof to each other. There is a lot of squealing and laughing while they do this.

When the bell rings, indicating that lunch hour is over, we all hurry in for the afternoon session. Mrs. Steinbach hands out the books and other supplies each of us will need. Time goes quickly and she decides to let school out a little early so she can get things in order for the next few days. Before we run home, Marjorie and I test out the new merry-go-round with a couple of spins. Then I say maybe we should go home by way of Grandma's house and see if she has a couple of sugar cookies for us. She doesn't disappoint and, munching on those big delicious cookies, we finally head back to the farm house.

The first thing I do, of course, is take off those high top shoes. As much as I like them, I am happy to be barefoot again. I end the summer as I began it, skipping barefoot down the lane, in the dusty path, whistling as I go. The summer is all but forgotten now. As I approach the wood lot, that same old crow announces my coming from the top of a tree. The cows head from the pasture to the barn, as they have all summer. They enter the barn yard and, before I close the gate, I take a couple more last steps in the soft, dry dirt of the path.

Chapter Thirteen

October has arrived. We have been harvesting and storing food all throughout the summer—Mother has been canning peas and green beans, strawberries, cherries, peaches and apples as they have ripened—but now the fall harvest season is here. A few days ago, when we heard frost warnings on the radio from Detroit's WWJ, we picked all the tomatoes still remaining on the vines. Mother canned the ripe ones and we wrapped the green ones in newspapers and stored them in the basement. Soon we'll pick all the squash and pumpkins and bury them in the wheat in the granary. They'll keep that way for months.

We also harvested the corn last month, both the field corn for the animals and the sweet corn for us. I helped Father drive the horses as they pulled the corn binder, a machine very similar to the wheat binder. We cut down the corn and he set up corn shocks in the field, just like we did with the wheat shocks earlier in the summer. After the corn shocks dried in the field, we hauled them to the barn. Next month the Parker brothers will come with their tractor and corn husker and shredder machine which will separate the ears of corn from the stalks in a process very similar to the way the wheat was separated from the straw. The corn will all go into a wagon, we'll pull it over to the corn crib, and shovel the corn into the crib. The shredder will also cut up the corn stalks and blow them into a mow in the barn for winter feed for the cows.

We harvested the turnips and carrots too, though we left some carrots in the ground and covered them with straw. That way the ground won't freeze and we'll be able to dig fresh carrots even at Christmastime.

A few weeks ago Father dug up the potato vines with a digging fork, and separated the potatoes from the root system. After we allowed them to dry in the field for a few hours, I helped pick them up and put them into wooden bushel crates. We carried the crates to the barn and sorted the potatoes, one by one. The best ones we put aside to sell, the bad ones we fed to the animals, and the rest we carried to the vegetable cellar, in the basement of our house. We stored them there along with apples and pears that we'd picked from the old orchard across the highway. The apples filled the small storage room with a wonderful smell.

In one corner of the vegetable cellar we piled some huge heads of cabbage, harvested from Grandpa's garden. Those are for sauerkraut. To make sauerkraut, we first shred the cabbage, pushing the heads over a wide wooden board that has a couple of sharp metal blades embedded in it. Just past the blades, there is an opening in the board that allows the shredded cabbage to fall through into a large clay crock beneath. Every so often Father removes the shredder board and asks me to tamp the shredded cabbage firmly into the crock with a wooden mallet, to be sure that the cabbage and salt, which we add frequently, are completely compacted. When the large crock is completely filled, we close it with a round wooden cover that fits just inside the lip, then we lay a heavy round field stone on top. The cabbage and salt mixture will ferment and turn into delicious sauerkraut over the next two months. We probably won't wait that long though. In about six weeks we'll be impatient to try it. We've made enough to last all winter. When it gets too strong, late in the winter, we'll just rinse it a little and it will still be delicious.

The fresh pork, the perfect meal with the sauerkraut, comes from one of the pigs we raised during the summer. Butchering time is in late November. It's a big event on the farm and everyone in the family is involved in some way. Grandpa and Uncle Herbert also come to help, and Uncle Herbert always brings a pig to be butchered along with ours.

Father and I herd the pig to be butchered from the pig yard to the back of the tool shed where a couple of strong poles are embedded in the ground. They are about six feet apart and a heavy wooden bar is fastened across their tops. After Grandpa kills the pigs with his twenty-two, they are hoisted with a rope and pulley by their rear legs, so they hang head down from this wooden bar. Grandpa then makes deep cuts in their necks, piercing the main artery and allowing all the blood to drain out on the ground. This is done to make certain the meat will be a nice pink color and more tasty when cooked. If the blood is left in, the meat will turn black.

While all this is happening, a big fire is roaring nearby and a huge cast iron cauldron, filled with water, is balanced on three rocks above the flames. We pour the boiling water over the pigs, cleaning them and also scalding their skins to make it easier to scrape off their rough, stiff hair. We all get to help with the scraping. The scraping tool is a saucer shaped metal piece, sharpened around the edge, embedded in a short wooden handle. I need both hands to hold one, but Father sometimes scrapes with one in each hand.

When all the hair is scraped off, the pigs are rinsed one final time with more hot water, and then Grandpa makes a long incision from the neck to the area between the back legs. Now all the insides are visible and Grandpa reaches in with both hands and pulls them all away from the body and into a large metal tub on the ground, directly below the pig's head. The tub is then put aside, next to a bench we've brought out from the basement of the house. Mother removes the heart and liver, and carries them to the kitchen in a small metal container. There she will wash and cut them up and cook them. We'll have them for supper tonight, and whatever is left Mother will store in the ice box and we'll finish them over the next few days.

The intestines are salvaged from the tub and cleaned and scrubbed and placed in a small crock for making sausages later in the day.

Grandpa then cuts the pigs' heads from the bodies using a heavy meat knife and sometimes a meat saw. It is hard work. Then he carries the heads to the nearby bench and cuts off all the usable parts, the tongues, cheeks and ears. Mother cuts these up too, into fine pieces, and makes them into a tasty meat loaf called head cheese. After they are cooked they are great with pancakes, or in sandwiches.

Then Uncle Herbert cuts up the rest of his pig while Father cuts up ours. They cut the shoulder pieces off, then the rib area and finally the back legs. They will become the smoked hams. All the small scrap pieces from trimming the shoulders, legs, ribs, and back legs are put aside to grind into sausage meat later. The other good pieces of meat that are left, including the meat from around the pork chop bones—the very best of the entire pig—Mother will can.

The fat is then trimmed from the big parts of meat and made into lard. First the fat is cut into small pieces and cooked in the cauldron kettle. Cooking the fat renders the lard from the fiber contained in the fat and, after the hot liquid lard is strained through cheese cloth, what is left is what we call crackles. And are they good! The lard itself is stored in small crocks and will be used as shortening in making pies and for other cooking during the winter months.

Now it's time to make the sausages. Father gets the bowl of cleaned intestines and carefully rubs them with a light coating of salt. This will help to preserve the finished product. First, all the meat is ground in a hand cranked meat grinder. I get to turn the crank. When the scraps are all ground, the meat is mixed with just the right amount of salt, pepper, sage and a hint of garlic. Then comes the mixing. Father mixes and mixes with both hands. He says it's not mixed enough until it comes off your hands, leaving them clean, until it doesn't stick to them anymore.

Grandpa has brought a special device he uses to fill the intestines with the sausage meat. It's a round cast iron container with a small tube coming out of a hole in the side near the bottom. The scraps of meat go in the crock and one end of the intestines are fastened to the tube. Then the top is placed on the crock. There is a crank built into the top and, when I turn it, it pushes the top down into the crock, compressing the meat and squeezing it out the tube, filling the sausage like it was a snake.

Grandpa deftly ties off six inch sections of the filled intestines, called casings, to form the long sausage links you see in stores. But, there is nothing to compare with home made sausages.

The hams and shoulders are all trimmed then and made ready for soaking in a saltpeter solution for a few hours, to help preserve the meat. Tomorrow morning they will be hung in the small smoke house Father has built for this purpose. The smoke house is about the size and shape of a fishing shanty, four feet square, and six feet tall. There are round bars near the top from which to hang the meat. In a large metal tub, sitting on the ground inside the smoke house, we will build a small fire using green hickory wood that will make a lot of smoke. The meat will hang in the smoke house for a day or two, it will turn a rich brown color, and the smoking will preserve it for the winter months. When it's done, we'll hang the meat in the granary in the barn and the smoked hams will last till Easter. The outsides of the meat will turn all moldy and green over the winter, but once that's trimmed off, the insides will still be pink and delicious.

The harvest season has come to a close. We will eat well this winter.

Chapter Fourteen

My second cousin, Ronald Schairer, was here a few weeks ago. He lives with his family on the farm directly east of ours. Even though it was cold, he rode his new bike over, and showed me how to ride it too. I climbed on and he held the seat and the handlebars and ran next to me while I coasted down the driveway a few times. I soon got the hang of balancing and pedaling and then we took turns riding in the yard for the rest of the afternoon. I've wanted a bike for awhile too. What fun it would be to ride it around the farm and on the dirt roads in the neighborhood. And, in a few years, when the time comes for me to go to Dexter High, I could even use it to ride to school.

But, it's the 1930s, the time of the Great Depression. A bike costs money and money is hard to come by. Still, there are some ways that a farm boy like me can make a little money.

Every spring I've been helping Grandpa with his garden and berry patch. Grandpa's strawberries and raspberries grow near the highway and beginning in June his little stand is loaded with berry boxes full of strawberries, and soon after with raspberries. The stand looks real inviting to travelers along the highway, and many stop to buy. I help Grandpa pick the berries. I get to eat mouth watering berries right from the plants and I get paid for what I pick—all of 2 1/2 cents a quart! Grandpa never minds how much I eat while I pick, but I don't get paid for what I eat! If I make fifty cents a day, I am very happy. It all goes into my little bank for the bike.

In the winters I make a little money by starting the fire in the schoolhouse stove every morning. Since our family lives close to the school, I run over there first thing every morning, get a good fire going, then run back and eat breakfast. By the time Marjorie and I go back to school at nine, the room is nice and warm for everyone.

But I will make most of my money by fur trapping in the fall and winter months. Since I am in school all day, my trapping time is either before or after school hours. And, only after I finish my other farm chores.

A lot of the boys I know also trap fox, raccoon, muskrat, weasel, skunk, mink and opossums for their furs. We only trap in the winter months because winter fur is thicker, and more valuable than summer fur.

I got the idea for trapping on a visit to Grandpa after school one November day in that year of 1932. He was working at his tool bench in the new garage he'd built for his Model A Ford. After I greeted him I noticed some leg traps hanging from big nails on the side of the garage. I recognized what they were from conversations with my friends at school and I asked Grandpa if he ever used those traps. "Not for a long time now," he answered. Seeing a way I might make some more money to save for my bike, I quickly asked if he would let me use them, and would he teach me how.

"I figure you're getting old enough to do some trapping," he says. Right then and there, that afternoon, he and I gather together his dozen or so traps, along with some wire we'd use to fasten the short lightweight chain attached to the traps to a tree or a big fallen limb in the woods. Then Grandpa teaches me everything I'll need to know to start trapping. He shows me how to bait the traps with a dead chicken. That bait works well, he says, for all the animals, except muskrat. Muskrats love water and that means I'd need to place the traps in the stream. In the winter, with the water cold and icy, that's pretty uncomfortable, he says. So I may not want to pursue them very often.

Grandpa tells me how to find good places to set my traps; how to look in the wood lot for signs where a raccoon, skunk, or opossum might have moved about. "Once there will be snow on the ground," he says, "it will be easier to track the animals, but then many of them don't move around much in the winter. Skunks lie low and only come out if we have a January thaw or some warm winter weather."

I listen carefully, thank him a lot, and take the traps with me when I leave. The next day, after school, I head for our wood lot with my traps and wire and bait, a dead chicken I talked Mother into giving me, for my first trapping expedition. I find a place near the wood lot fence, where the dry, fall grass has been slightly beaten down. It looks like a path that has been used by one or more animals. A tall oak tree grows close by and one of its branches hangs out over the spot where the path goes through the fence. With a piece of wire, I hang the chicken from the branch, so it hangs a couple of feet above the ground. Then I set three traps below the chicken, and attach each of them to a heavy limb on the ground with more wire. I set the triggers on the traps, just like Grandpa showed me, being very careful not to catch my thumb or fingers in the traps. Then I cover them with some dry grass and leaves. If a raccoon, skunk or opossum steps on one, trying to reach the chicken overhead, it will trigger the trap.

I place several of these stations in the woods. I put one trap in a hole in the ground near the fence, which might be the home of one of these animals. Usually, it turns out to be just a rabbit den. That's fine too. If I catch a rabbit, it's meat for the table.

After I have set all my traps, I head back to the barn to help Father with the usual evening chores, then supper and bed. I am quite tired from setting the traps and doing chores.

The next morning I rise early to check my trap line before breakfast and school. I walk quickly to the barn yard, out into the lane, and into the wood lot. No more going barefoot now. It's November, cold and windy, and there is a heavy mist in the air. My high top shoes feel really good as I walk along the path.

At the hole in the ground by the wood lot fence the trap is undisturbed. I continue on to the chicken-baited station, by the big oak tree. The chicken is no longer hanging over the traps, but is laying on the ground. And, there is a strong smell of skunk in the air. Did I catch a skunk, I wonder excitedly. Sure enough, near where the chicken had been hanging, I spot a big black and white skunk, with its front leg caught in the trap, trying to get away. But he can only drag the trap, attached to the piece of tree limb, a little way into the woods. Now what do I do?

Remembering Grandpa's advice, I check the direction the wind is coming from and make sure I approach the skunk with the wind at my back. That way, if he sprays, the wind will carry the scent away from me. It's quite windy this morning, which helps.

I don't have a gun with me. A gun would allow me to kill it quickly without getting close, but a bullet hole in the fur and skin would decrease its value. So, I pick up a tree limb, about the size of a baseball bat, and slowly approach the skunk. Still keeping the wind at my back I draw nearer and nearer to my target.

The skunk watches me warily as I creep closer. When I am close enough, I raise the stick high and bring it down sharply on the skunk's head. Then I jump back, turn, and run a short ways away, into the wind. Grandpa has warned me to do this, because a skunk emits a great deal of strong odor in its last moments. Hopefully, the wind will blow it away from me.

When I see that the skunk is dead, I quickly check the other stations. None of them are disturbed. I am relieved. One skunk will be enough to deal with. I hurry back to take the dead skunk from the trap. I do this very carefully, trying not to get any of the strong skunk odor on myself. I tie the skunk to the end of a long stick, reset the traps, and hang the remnants of the chicken back on the tree limb. Then, resting the stick with the skunk attached on my shoulder, I head for home.

Back at the house, I wash myself as well as I can and put on clean clothes, but despite my efforts, when I get to school, everyone knows what I caught this morning.

66

After school, I skin the skunk. It's not a pleasant task, but necessary if I am to sell the fur. Grandpa shows me how to do this as well. First, he tells me, I need to make sure my trusty Boy Scout knife is very sharp. I pull it from its holder on the side of my high top shoe and run into the tool shed to hone it on Father's sharpening stone. While I'm in there, I also grab a hammer and some nails. We take the skunk to the back of the tool shed and drive two nails into the boards that make up the back of the shed. Following Grandpa's instructions, I tie the rear legs of the skunk to the two nails with a bit of cord, the back of the skunk against the boards and its belly facing me.

Next, I make a few quick cuts with my knife around the ankle bones of the rear legs and then a swift cut through the skin between the legs, just to the flesh of the body. By carefully cutting a strip of the hide away from the flesh of each of the legs I can grasp these strips and slowly, but forcefully, pull the hide away from the legs and gradually from the entire body of the skunk, the way you'd pull a heavy sweater over your head. I end up with the skin and fur off the skunk and inside out.

Grandpa and I then make a stretching board. We find a wooden board about six, eight inches wide and eighteen inches long and, using a draw shave, a tool that looks like a large knife blade with a handle at each end, we work one end of the board into a dome shape, to fit the smaller end of the fur where the head had been. When the stretching board is done I carefully pull the top of the hide over the shaped end, stretch it as tight as I can and fasten it to the other end of the board with a couple nails through the hide where the back legs had been. I hang the board from a nail on the inside wall of the tool shed so the fur can dry out. Late in the winter, the fur buyer will stop by. He'll pay one or two dollars for skunk and opossum hides, four or five dollars for raccoon and as much as twenty dollars for mink. Mink are pretty rare around here. Maybe I will catch more in my traps by then and I can sell him my furs and put away more money towards my bike.

Needless to say, after I am finished stretching the skin, I need another good hot, soapy bath.

Chapter Fifteen

Christmas is coming! Always a special time of year, and especially for our family. It was five years ago, just before Christmas, when I was five years old, that we moved into our new farmhouse. The new house was our giant Christmas present that year. Our whole family was very excited about the move. We all still remember it, especially at Christmas time.

It was the first time we had indoor plumbing and electricity. How nice it was to be able to take baths in a nice new bathtub, instead of in our well-used old wash tub at the old house. How nice not to have to go out back to the outhouse on cold January evenings. How nice to be able to turn on electric lights with just the flick of a switch, rather than fuss with kerosene lantern wicks.

The house in which I was born. Note the outhouse in the lower left corner.

Our old house was just across the highway from our new one. I was born in that house and, when I started walking, Mother began worrying about the highway. Would I be safe, crossing back and forth to our farm and fields on the north side of US 12? Almost all the automotive traffic that went from Detroit to Chicago drove on that road. So, Father and Mother began planning a new house near our barn and other farm buildings on the north side of the highway.

One of Father's cousins who lived in Ann Arbor was a builder, and he and his crew built our new house. Father and Uncle Herbert worked right alongside them and did a lot of the rough carpentry. Even I got to help a little. One time Father let me use a hammer to help him drive some nails, fastening wood lath for plaster, to the wall studding in one of the closets.

The living room in our new house is much larger than in our old one. It also has a beautiful brick fireplace with an oak mantel and stone faced hearth. However, much to Mother's disappointment, it sometimes allows wood smoke to blow back into the

Our freshly built new house. Notice that there are no trees near it.

room if the wind isn't just right over the top of the chimney. A mistake in the chimney construction is to blame. But, if we are careful, and don't build too big a fire, we can occasionally enjoy that fireplace. And Christmas Eve is always one of those special occasions.

We spend almost the whole day of Christmas Eve decorating. First, Father brings down from the attic our much loved, antique Christmas tree stand. It was brought here from Germany more than fifty years ago, by some relatives of Grandpa. It used to be in Grandma and Grandpa's house, but it's been in our house ever since I can remember. Every Christmas it takes its honored place next to the fireplace at the west end of our living room. The tree stand is about two feet wide and three feet long. The back end is about a foot higher than the front, and

70

there is a rounded terrace scene leading up from the front to the back. On the back end, at the higher elevation, there is a replica of an old German country house. It is made of metal, painted light brown, with black trim on the windows and door. It has a large verandah in front, an arched roof at the top and, of course, a chimney for Old Saint Nick to use on Christmas Eve. Next to the house, fitted into the wooden base, is a piece of iron pipe, which can hold a small Christmas tree.

Our Christmas tree stand.

At the lower end of the stand, at the bottom of the terrace, is a small oval-shaped metal pool with a fountain in the center. We pour water for the fountain into a small tank in the top of the house, under the roof. There is a small rubber tube running from the tank, underneath the stand, to the fountain. At the center of the pond stands a beautiful angel figure poised on a pedestal, wings extended and right arm raised above her head. Coming out of her hand is the end of the tube through which the water bubbles and falls into the pool with a soft murmuring sound. The water then drains into a pail under the stand. It takes maybe fifteen minutes for all the water from the tank to come through the fountain. I love pulling the bucket out from under the stand, refilling the tank at the top, and watching and listening as the fountain gurgles merrily.

The Christmas tree stand rests on a four legged bench that Father has made especially for this purpose. Every year Mother covers the bench with a pretty green colored cloth that hangs down all the way to the floor, hiding the pail that collects the water that drains from the fountain pool.

71

This morning, after chores, Father goes to the wood lot and cuts down a small evergreen tree that fits neatly into the pipe on the stand. Grandpa and I also go into the woods and we gather some green velvet-like moss from around the north side of tree stumps and big stones. We collect almost a full bushel basket of moss, all we can carry, and bring it back to the house.

We carefully place the moss on the surface of the tree stand to form a beautiful, natural looking green lawn around the house, terrace, and pool area.

Now the tree decorating can start. First, Mother puts some small candles into clip-on holders and attaches them to the branches of the Christmas tree. Once the candles are in place, it's time for the other decorations. Inside the little old German farmhouse we put a tiny table and chairs and some small ceramic figures, all dressed in colorful clothes, gathered around it. In the yard, around the house and on the moss covered terrace, we put miniature figures of sheep and cattle pasturing peacefully under the tree and down by the pond.

Mother brings out a box containing more decorations for the tree. There are shiny silver and gold balls we've used for years. She also unpacks a few little angels she's made from bits of cloth left over from her sewing projects. We hang these too and then she hands us a small box containing tinsel and we drape the shiny strands over the branches. Finally, she brings forth one more item to place on the very top of the tree. It's a beautiful, angel-shaped doll she has made just for the occasion.

It is now late in the afternoon, the tree is trimmed, and Father has the farm chores, milking the cows, feeding and checking on all the animals. Mother heads for the kitchen to prepare a bowl of scalloped oysters for tonight. The oysters and crackers are a special treat from my uncles' store in Chelsea. A loaf of her home made bread will round out our supper.

Grandpa and Grandma come over for the festive evening meal and then we gather in the living room by the Christmas tree. Father starts a fire in the fireplace. The wind cooperates and no smoke comes back into the house. I sit on the hearth, near the fireplace as everyone else gets comfortable in chairs. Father lights the candles on the tree while Mother stands nearby with a basin of water, just in case a lighted candle should fall over. We turn off the electric lights and sit quietly, enjoying the glow from the fire in the fireplace and the flickering light of the candles.

When the candles have burned down, Grandma suggests we sing Christmas carols. Father gets his violin, tunes up, and we start singing the familiar songs. We end with Silent Night in German. All the adults know how to speak German, though they rarely do, but I don't know the language almost at all. Before World War I, many people around here spoke German. It was even taught in our Country School, but that stopped during the war. My folks have never taught us any German and so Marjorie, Lloyd and I are the only ones not singing along on Silent Night tonight.

Our fireplace at Christmastime.

After the caroling it's time to open some presents! Marjorie and I excitedly unwrap a checkerboard from Grandma and Grandpa and a domino set from Mother and Father. There is Mother's homemade chocolate fudge with walnuts and hickory nuts from our own trees. Grandma has made her delicious lebkuchen, German ginger cookies, and each of us kids get a specially wrapped mouth-watering orange, a rare treat and a traditional Christmas gift from Grandma and Grandpa that we look forward to every year.

Mother has made a whole family of pretty rag dolls for Marjorie, and Father brings up my gift from the basement. It is a small workbench he has built from scratch. Made of pine, the perfect size for

73

my height, it's very sturdy and has a drawer and a wooden vise. I can't believe my good fortune. Now I'll be able to do my little woodworking projects on my own workbench.

The fire has died down and is now just a small mound of glowing embers. It's getting late and the farm chores will need to be done early tomorrow morning, Christmas or not. We exchange cheery Christmas wishes with Grandma and Grandpa and they head back to their home across the highway. Mother puts Lloyd to bed and Marjorie and I hurry to hang our Christmas stockings on the fireplace mantel before we head upstairs. It takes me a long time to fall asleep, wondering when Santa will come and what he will bring.

Chapter Sixteen

Christmas and the New Year's holiday week is over. The month of January is upon us. It is time to go to the wood lot and cut wood for next year's heating season. Father and Uncle Herbert have started doing this together earlier in the week, but since today is Saturday and I have no school, I get to go with Father and help.

It's very cold this morning, below zero. But, the sky is blue and there's no wind. Father says if we dress warmly, and work hard, we'll stay warm. He also tells Mother that he will build a little fire in the wood lot to warm our hands and feet if we get really cold.

After morning chores and breakfast, we go to the barn, harness the horses, Topsy and Buster, and hitch them to the sleigh we use to haul logs from the wood lot to the farm yard. I'm wearing an extra pair of woolen socks inside my high top shoes, and a thick sweater and wool jacket Mother made for me. Father has brought along our big horse blanket to help fend off the cold. Made from the

Our house in the snow.

hide and fur of a horse, with a thick wool lining, the blanket is very heavy. It's been in our family for a long time. Father says he remembers that when he and Uncle Herbert were little boys, they kept warm under that same blanket, sitting between Grandma and Grandpa as they all traveled by horse and buggy or, when there was snow, by sleigh, in the days before cars came along. As he tells the story, I can almost see him and Uncle Herbert huddling beneath that blanket on their way to church on a Christmas morning many years ago.

Sure enough, between the horse blanket and all the clothes I'm wearing, I am comfortable on our journey down the lane to the wood lot.

And here we are, entering the woods. The snow is about eight inches deep and the sleigh creaks and the runners squeak and hiss as Topsy and Buster pull us over the snow covered ground, their breathing creating white clouds in the cold air.

On the east side of the wood lot, where the sun is now shining brightly, we stop by a big oak tree that Father decides will make good firewood for next season. It's at least two feet in diameter. We unload the axes, cross cut saw and a heavy maul Father uses to drive steel wedges into the logs we will be cutting soon. That's how he will split them into smaller pieces so they can be loaded onto the sleigh and hauled back to the farm yard and eventually cut into firewood chunks. After we've unloaded the tools, Father drives Topsy and Buster a little ways away and ties them to another tree while we cut down the oak he's selected.

Before we start sawing, Father finds a few pieces of dead wood sticking up through the snow and arranges them to make a nice fire to warm our hands and feet later. We then head over to where we've left the saw, ax and maul. After walking around the big oak, and studying the nearby trees, Father decides that the tree can fall in a southerly direction, between the other trees, and avoid any damage to them. He picks up the ax and chops a V shaped notch about sixteen inches above the ground, into the side of the tree trunk facing the direction in which he wants it to fall.

We then pick up the saw and start sawing on the side of the tree opposite from the notch Father has made with the ax. The saw is about five feet long, six inches wide and almost an eighth of an inch thick, with lots of sharp teeth cut into one edge of the blade. It has a short handle, about a foot long, on each end of the blade which Father and I grasp as we pull the saw back and forth. The sharp teeth bite into the wood and each stroke sends a stream of yellow sawdust into the fresh snow on the ground.

It takes a lot of effort and time to cut through the big tree. When I get tired and my hands and feet get cold, I stop pulling on the saw and ask if we can go over by the fire to get warm. Father agrees and we stand by the warm fire for a short break. Then it's back to work.

We are sawing in a nice rhythmical manner, when suddenly I hear a tremendous boom echoing through the stillness of the wood lot!

"What was that?" I exclaim, and stop pulling on the saw. Father suggests we rest a little again and while we stand by the fire he tells me he thinks that the booming noise came from one of the large oak trees along the east side of the wood lot. The bright January sun, shining on the east side of the tree, caused that side to thaw faster than the west side, still in the shade. The quick thawing from the heat of the sun made the bark and outer wood fibers expand rapidly, causing the wood and bark to crack suddenly, producing the big boom we heard.

We stand by the fire for a bit, and I keep thinking about that strange booming sound. Finally Father says maybe we should get back to sawing on the tree.

After another ten minutes of sawing, Father tells me to go and stand by the horses. We are getting close to sawing through the trunk and when the tree falls, he tells me, it might scare the horses. I know he's really more concerned about me than the horses. They've been through this experience many times before. But I go and stand by Topsy and Buster, and put my hand on Topsy's shoulder. Father makes a few more cuts by himself, and suddenly I hear a faint cracking sound, and the tree starts to fall in the direction Father planned. Father quickly runs behind a nearby tree and we watch as the tree falls. It falls swiftly. The upper branches, leafless now, swish through the cold air and as they hit the ground stir up a huge cloud of dry cold snow just before the heavy trunk of the tree hits the frozen ground with a loud thumping, thudding sound. Then, once again, as the cloud of snow settles back to earth, the woods are silent. Topsy and Buster take all this in stride, not moving, as I lean against them, taking it all in.

I walk back to where Father is standing, looking at the fallen tree. He checks his pocket watch and says it's almost time to go back to the house for dinner, but first maybe we could trim a few branches from the trunk. We each pick up an ax and start chopping the limbs from the tree trunk, working mostly near the top of the tree. Father tells me to throw the branches I'm cutting far enough away from the trunk, so later we'll have room to stand on each side of the log and saw it into six foot lengths. That will make it easier to split the logs into thinner pieces and load them onto the sleigh.

After a little while Father says it is time to leave the woods and go back to dinner. He brings the horses back and I climb aboard the sleigh for the ride back to the house. Much warmer now, from all the work, I enjoy the trip. Father says that after dinner I can stay in the house and rest, or play with Marjorie. That sounds good to me.

Chapter Seventeen

Father and Uncle Herbert, with a little help from me on Saturdays, have continued cutting and splitting more tree logs in the past couple of months. (Of course, its not been all work and no play for me. Whenever there's been enough snow, Marjorie and I have gone sledding.) We've hauled the logs back to the farm yard on the sleigh, to join the logs we brought in earlier woodcutting sessions. We've stacked the split logs, along with smaller and longer pieces from tree limbs, to form a large pile of wood, shaped like a huge loaf of bread, covering a space at least twenty five feet long and twenty feet wide, behind the garage and tool shed, to await "buzzing," being cut into stove length pieces.

And now it's March, the month of spring. Time to buzz up that stack of wood. A few days ago Father called Mr. Parker, a neighbor farmer who owns the only buzz saw rig in the area, who agreed to come today, Saturday. I'm excited; that means I will be around to watch. Father has also called Uncle Herbert and a couple of other neighbors to help. It takes four or five people to buzz wood properly. It's really hard work.

We do the morning chores, as usual, and just as we finish cooling the milk, the buzz saw rig arrives, pulled by a tractor. It reminds me of when the summer threshing machine came, but this is a much smaller tractor and machine. This tractor can also be used for plowing and tilling ground. It's the only one like it in the neighborhood. The rest of the farms still use only horses for these tasks.

It doesn't take long to set up for sawing. Mr. Parker pulls into our yard, unhitches the saw rig from the tractor draw bar, turns the tractor around so it's facing the rig, attaches a long belt between the pulley on the rig and one on the tractor and we are ready to saw the wood.

The buzzing rig is a large circular saw blade nearly a yard in diameter, mounted on a wooden frame. The saw is turned by the belt leading to the tractor in the same way the threshing machine ran. The rig has a table top that can move back and forth on the framework that the saw is mounted on. This allows the man running the saw rig to push the long pieces of wood into the rapidly turning saw blade, cutting them into pieces about sixteen to twenty inches long, the size needed to burn in a furnace or stove.

Uncle Herbert and couple of other neighbors arrive and things begin to happen. Mr. Parker engages the pulley with a lever and releases the clutch on the tractor. The belt begins to turn the saw blade faster and faster and faster until it emits an eerie high-pitched whistling sound. The men bring the logs to Mr. Parker one at a time and help hold them on the table while he pushes the logs into the whirling blade. One man stands next to the saw frame and takes each sawed off chunk and tosses it off to the side. By late afternoon, when all the wood is sawed, there will be a huge pile of chunks there.

The sound of the saw blade teeth cutting through the wood sends a shrill sound into the air that can be heard from far away. All the farm neighbors know we are buzzing wood. It's also very dusty, dirty work. The sawdust falls to the ground and bounces back into the air around those working near the saw. It can get in your eyes and nose and be very irritating. But the work has to be done, and I get nearly as dirty as the men because I like to watch from up close.

After a couple of hours the men take a break and Father brings out a big pot of coffee and a jug of water to wash away the dust in our throats. He also brings a couple of towels to wipe away the sawdust from our faces. Then it's back to work. The stack of logs is almost half gone, and the pile of chunks is pretty big when it's time to stop for dinner.

Before going into the house, we all take turns and, with a couple of brooms, sweep the sawdust off each other. Then we wash our hands and faces in the washroom next to the kitchen, with water that's been heated by an iron pipe coil in the kitchen stove and stored in a tank near the sink.

Mother has cooked up a good hot dinner for us all, similar to the one in the summer when we threshed the wheat. In the cool March weather, the good hot meal goes over big with everyone.

Then, back to sawing wood. In about two more hours of sawing, the job is finished. Mr. Parker hooks up his rig and heads for home, along with the other neighbors who helped. Father goes to the barn to do the evening chores, but I stay and play around in the huge pile of fresh sawdust, the pungent odor of fresh-sawed wood filling the cool late afternoon springtime air.

Out of the corner of my eye, I am aware of the enormous pile of sawed wood and know I will have to help Father move all those chunks to the woodshed before next winter. We'll do this by loading them on our wagon, then the horses will pull the wagon to the woodshed where it will be my job to unload and stack the chunks in neat rows in the shed.

I put the thought of all that work out of my mind for now though, and head for the house to await supper. Marjorie, Lloyd and I listen to Amos and Andy on the radio while Father finishes the milking, and then we have supper.

It's Saturday night. That means a bath is in order. But, in our nice bathtub, it's more fun than in the washtub I still remember from our old house. Then we're off to bed, tired from the day of wood buzzing. Tomorrow is Sunday. We'll drive to Chelsea in our still new car, go to church, and visit Grandma Hinderer.

Chapter Eighteen

It is now early in the month of May and we are right in the middle of planting season for corn, and also fast approaching the last of Country School days for the summer.

I am now old enough to do more work around the farm. This Saturday, just before summer vacation starts, Father tells me I can do some plowing for him. I like that idea and go with him to harness the horses and hook them up to our one bottom plow. I climb up on the plow's seat, take the reins, and we head down the driveway to the field across Parker Road. The iron wheels, attached to the plow frame, make crunching sounds as we cross the gravel road.

Once in the field I drive the horses to where Father had stopped plowing yesterday. What a contrast between the half that he plowed, with its nice dark-brown furrows, and the half that I will be plowing today, green with grass and weeds and the remnants of last summer's hay, trying to make a comeback this spring.

We've hitched three horses to the plow, Buster, Flori and Topsy. They are well trained in the all tasks they are asked to do. Buster on the left, the only male, has a tendency to be rather lazy, but the other two are very energetic. Topsy, in the middle, is the leader of the team. She knows what has to be done and lets the other two know if they aren't doing their part in the work by giving them a quick bite with her front teeth now and then. That's a fact! I am not kidding. Buster, on her right, walks in the furrow, the small ditch left by the plow on the previous round.

I turn the horses to the right and head north across the field.

The ride on this nice May morning is quiet and smooth as the plow turns the good earth beneath me. Occasionally, of course, we hit a stone underground and that jars the plow, and me, considerably. But still, it's a great experience for me. As we go back and forth across the field I can hear the birds singing once again, now that spring is in full bloom. On one of the trips around I look up into the bright blue sky and see my two favorite turkey buzzards sailing along on the spring breeze as they did last year.

It's the middle of the morning now and I am getting a bit hungry. At the south end of the field, across the street car tracks and the highway, is our country store. I decide to stop there. I tie the horses to a fence post, climb the fence, cross the tracks and the highway and go into the store. I have five cents in my overall pocket and that's just enough to buy a Baby Ruth candy bar. I hurry back to the horses, untie them and start back across the field, munching on that delicious candy bar.

We make several more rounds across the field when I hear the sound of an airplane engine overhead. It's a United Airlines DC 3, the new passenger plane from Detroit to Chicago. It is beautiful with its two engines, one on each side of the cabin, set in the wings. I watch as it disappears into the western sky, wishing I could be on it. Maybe I would feel as free as those turkey buzzards I saw earlier.

That plane is always on time. It passes over our farm every day at exactly 11:30 AM, so I never need a watch to know how close it's getting to dinner time.

I turn the team toward home when suddenly I hear buzzing around my head and face and feel a sharp pain as something stings me. At the same time, the horses start jumping, kicking and running. There are bees all around us now. The plow starts bouncing wildly as the horses gallop and I get thrown off onto the soft, plowed ground. I am not hurt, but the bees are still trying to sting me. I flail my hands and arms around and run as fast as I can after the horses. They have been stung by the bees also. By the time I catch up to them, and finally leave the bees behind, we're almost to the gate leading out of the field. The bumblebees must have headed back to their destroyed nest that the plow turned upside down. A distressing event for all concerned.

I climb back onto the plow seat and, after a few soothing and encouraging words to the horses, we head for the barn. Father meets us there and we unhitch the horses and lead them to the water tank for a drink. Then we put them in their stalls for dinner, a pail of oats and a fork full of hay from last summer's hay crop.

Then we too head in to dinner. On the way, I tell Father about the bees. He suggest that maybe I should take the afternoon off and have some fun after such an experience. I gratefully accept his offer and we go into the house for another good meal, and then a fun afternoon with Marjorie and Lloyd.

Chapter Nineteen

There is more to getting a field ready for planting corn, than just plowing. Father has finished the plowing during the week and today, another Saturday, I am again not in school and so can help him with "fitting" the ground for the planting of the seed corn.

We once again harness the horses. This time we use only two, Flori and Topsy. They will pull the land roller to compact the rough furrows left by the plow. The roller is a heavy metal cylinder about eight feet wide and a yard in diameter with a wooden frame and a seat for the driver. After we hitch the horses to the roller, I climb on that seat and we head for the freshly plowed field.

It is a noisy, bumpy ride down the driveway, but when we enter the field and pull onto the soft, plowed earth, the noise subsides and the ride softens as we roll and level those furrows. The horses hooves sink deep into the soft earth and they seem to enjoy that feeling the same way I like walking barefoot in the deep dust of the cow path.

It's another beautiful warm spring day. I look behind me occasionally to watch the roller doing it's work, and I listen to its soft thumping sounds mixed in with the music of the birds. The bees have not returned to their destroyed nest since last week and they don't bother me.

The rolling goes much faster than the plowing did. After a couple of hours the field is almost half done. I decide to once again stop near the country store, and tie the horses to the fence. I make a beeline for the candy counter for another Baby Ruth candy bar. After paying the five cents, I turn and start for the front door when I notice that the doorway to the basement is open. I remember Burton and his basement project. Burton Murray is the younger son of Mr. Murray, the man who owns the country store. He is about twenty years old and for the past year has been building an actual airplane down there. I have found my way down those stairs plenty of times before.

I know Burton has been getting close to completing that airplane, but when I reach the bottom step, what a sight greets my eyes! There it is, practically ready to fly. The bright red fuselage stands on its two front wheels and tail skid. The wings, in two sections each, lean against the basement wall, ready to be mounted on struts directly above the cockpit. Burton, beaming proudly, asks me what I think of it.

I am practically speechless with excitement, but finally manage to stammer something, and he tells me that next week he will take it out of the basement, put the wings on and fly it from the big field behind the store.

"Field?! The horses!" I have completely forgotten about them, and that I am supposed to be rolling the ground! I sprint up the stairs, hurry out the door, back across the highway and tracks where the horses are tied to the fence. Thank goodness, they are still waiting for me. Topsy whines at me to hurry. We have work to do. I untie them from the fence, climb on the roller seat, turn them around and we head off across the field.

Soon I hear that 11:30 D.C. 3 airliner heading for Chicago. It's almost dinner time. I watch the plane disappear in the western sky, take a couple more turns around the field, and then head the horses for the barn. When I have fed them their dinner, I go in the house for mine.

Well, Burton did try to fly that plane. I wasn't there, but I heard about it from Mr. Bradbury, the neighbor farmer whose field he used to try to take off. He attached the wings all right, and started the motorcycle engine he'd installed in the fuselage by turning the big propeller in the front. After idling and racing the engine for a few minutes, Burton removed a couple of big blocks he'd placed in front of the wheels and climbed into the cockpit. Mr. Bradbury told us that Burton then pushed the throttle open and taxied around the field a few times. Then, turning into the wind, he started across the field. When he was halfway across, the wheels left the ground and Burton was flying! But, he didn't get very high before something went wrong. Whether the engine quit, or Burton panicked, Mr. Bradbury didn't know. What he did see though is that the plane began to tip and dive and finally crashed, nose first, into the ground. The propeller, engine, and the front of the fuselage were all crumpled and smashed. Burton walked away with just a few bumps and bruises, but the plane was beyond repair. That was the end of that beautiful little airplane. Burton must have been very disappointed. He never again mentioned it.

Chapter Twenty

It rained last weekend, a much needed rain, and just in time for planting the corn seed. Before we can plant though, we still have to "drag" the plowed and rolled soil. Father does this with a tool called a spring tooth drag. The drag has a steel frame with metal runners, like a sled, and three cross bars going from one runner to the other. Each bar has a series of curved steel teeth that work up the rolled down earth and make it receptive to the corn seed.

The drag has no seat, so whoever drives the horses has to walk behind it. Walking in the soft, freshly dragged soil isn't too hard to do, especially barefoot. It can be a dusty job though, if the ground is dry, but the rain last weekend has made the ground just right for planting the seed, as well as for walking barefoot.

It usually takes two or three trips with the spring tooth drag over the plowed ground to properly prepare it for planting. Father did the dragging during the week and finished yesterday, Friday, so we would be ready to plant today, Saturday, when I am out of school.

Father has asked Uncle Herbert and Grandpa to also help us. When they arrive about nine o'clock, we already have the horses hitched to the planter, ready to roll. Uncle Herbert has brought with him a large roll of wire that has knots in it every forty inches. We'll be using that wire, along with our corn planter to plant the seed corn.

The roll of wire is quite heavy. It is wound on a wooden spool with an old broom handle through the center of it. Uncle Herbert and Grandpa carry it by holding the broom handle on either side of the spool.

We start by fastening one end of the wire to an iron stake that Father has driven into the ground at one end of the field. Then Uncle Herbert and Grandpa unroll the wire clear to the other end of the field, pull it as tight as they can and fasten it there to another stake.

We plant corn seed with a tool called a corn planter. It is a rather new invention. Like the roller I used last weekend, the corn planter also has a frame with two wheels and a seat, and is also pulled by two horses. The planter has a small round hopper at the top that the seed is placed in. There is also a device that hooks to the wire that we've stretched on the ground. The knots in that wire trip a mechanism in the bottom of the hopper that allows three or four corn seeds to drop down through a tube and into a steel runner that cuts into the ground about three inches deep. The wheels of the corn planter cover and compact the fresh soil around the corn seed as the planter moves along the field.

Father brings the horses and planter, hooks the wire into the trip mechanism on the seed hopper, and starts across the field. The knots in the wire set off a loud ticking sound as they trip the mechanism, allowing the few kernels of corn seed to drop into the ground. When the planter reaches the other end of the field, Uncle Herbert and Grandpa, at either end of the field, move the iron stakes forty two inches toward the opposite side of the field. This distance between the rows will allow the corn rows to be cultivated from both directions, to kill the weeds that will be growing later.

My job is to be in the middle of the field and help keep the wire in a nice straight line across the field. I don't have much time to rest, but occasionally I sit on the nice, soft earth and listen to the birds sing their bright, cheery springtime songs as they gather the materials to build their nests.

Here comes that 11:30 airliner, heading for Chicago again. That means it won't be long till dinner time. A couple more moves of the wire and we head for the farm house. Once again, Mother has a fine dinner prepared for us all. Marjorie helps by carrying some of the food to the table.

We all enjoy the meal and then head back to the field. By late afternoon we are done. We're all tired, including the horses, and glad the work is finished.

But, there is even more than this to raising corn. Once the corn starts growing, it has to be cultivated to control the inevitable weeds that will follow. The cultivator is similar to the corn planter, but has two devices connected to the frame, with several small shovel-like teeth that can be lowered into the ground to kill the weeds. The cultivating devices are mounted on each side of the frame and controlled by the feet of the driver. There is a space between them for the corn plants, so they are not destroyed along with the weeds. It's a great improvement, and time saver, over the use of a hoe to eliminate the weeds. It usually takes three cultivations, about a week apart, or until the corn becomes too tall to allow cultivation without harming the corn stalks.

Father doesn't let me cultivate the corn. He says I am too young yet, but my time will come in a few years.

The corn field is a great place for the killdeer to make their nest. The black birds like to pick the kernels of corn from the tips of the young ears of corn, as they are forming. The crows like to follow behind the corn planter and try to dig up the kernels of seed corn, much to Father's dismay. When the corn stalks reach maturity, six or seven feet tall, the field is a great place for Marjorie, Lloyd and me to play hide and seek. Also for deer to hide from hunters during the fall hunting season.

There is no more interesting crop than corn. Last summer, Grandpa told me that when the corn stalks grow quickly during warm, humid weather in July and August, you can actually hear them growing. It's true. One hot, still summer day I stood quietly in the field and could hear a faint snap, crackle and pop, as the stalks reached for the sky.

93

Chapter Twenty-One

Although, as Father says, I'm too young yet to cultivate the corn and do some of the other tasks around the farm, now that I'm eleven, a little older and stronger, there is more and more that I can do. I can help clean the horse stable and even harness the horses in the morning and unharness them at the end of the day's work. Those harnesses are still pretty heavy and clumsy for me to handle, but I work with them proudly.

The cow stables have to be kept clean too, both morning and evening after milking—every day. It's rather smelly work, but necessary, and it's not too hard to do with a fork and shovel and a bit of muscle.

Father also decides I can now feed the cows their ground up corn and oats every morning and evening. We grow all the corn and oats in our own fields and then Father takes a trailer load of ear corn and oats, pulls it with our car to the feed mill in Dexter and has it ground into mash. We store the ground-up feed in a large bin by the cow stable door. The grain bin is thirty or forty steps from the cow mangers, so it saves Father a considerable amount of time if I feed the cows.

Then there is the milking, every morning and evening, every day of the year, even Christmas! Father says that this summer I am old enough to help with that. Although I've seen him milk cows all my life, tonight he says he'll teach me how it's done.

When I have the cows from pasture, we let them into the cow stable and they each find their own special place in the row of stanchions in the barn. Cows are creatures of habit and we have little trouble training them to learn which stanchion is theirs.

With the cows latched securely in their stanchions and eating their ground feed, it's time for the milking. Father finds a small wooden box for me to use as a stool. He also brings me a nice shiny ten quart pail in which to `catch the milk.

I take the box in one hand, the pail in the other, and walk to my first cow. I sit down on the right side of the cow, just in front of the right rear leg. I place the pail between my knees and rest my forehead on the cow's side as I've seen Father do so many times before. I grasp two of the teats, one in each hand. With the cow happily eating her feed, I boldly squeeze my right hand tightly around the teat.

Nothing happens.

I try it with my left hand.

Still nothing.

I look at Father, very bewildered. He laughs and then explains that I must first squeeze the top of the teat with my thumb and first finger to close the little tube the milk comes through. Then I need to squeeze the rest of the teat.

I try that and when I squeeze my third finger around the teat, then the fourth and fifth, much to my delight, a stream of warm white milk hits the bottom of the shiny empty pail with a clear ringing sound. I try it with my left hand too. It works! I alternate squeezing with each hand, gradually finding the rhythm I've heard so often from Father, and I am milking my first cow!

I help Father with the milking of our dozen cows throughout the summer. Come fall, when school starts again, I'll only milk in the evenings and on the weekends when there is no school.

I don't know it at the time, but milking cows every day will be a big part of the rest of my life.

Epilogue

My memories of that year still remain vivid in my mind today, seventy five years later. Of course, much happened every day and every year as I grew older, but it is that year of 1932-1933, when I was ten and turned eleven, that I remember the best.

But, there are many other memories that have stayed with me from my childhood.

I attended confirmation classes in our church, St. Paul's Evangelical Lutheran, when I was twelve. They lasted from fall until Easter. Mother learned to drive our new car and every week she drove me the eight miles to Chelsea, for my class. In the winter, if the roads were bad, we rode the electric street car.

Our class had to memorize many Bible stories during those months. During the final examination we all had to be prepared to recite what we'd learned. I still retain many of those Bible stories to this day.

One Sunday we were studying about the first miracle of the Lord Jesus Christ. The story is in the Bible, in John 12-1-12. It occurred at a wedding feast when the hosts ran out of wine for the celebration. The story, as our minister, Reverend Paul Grabowski told it, was quite vivid and caught the attention of the class. He told how Jesus' Mother asked him if he couldn't do something about the problem. And, as the Bible relates, Jesus turned jars of water into wine, much to the amazement of all at the wedding party—and to mine as well. Because I recall leaning over to the classmate on my right and whispering, "Boy, I wish I knew what he did."

Well, you guessed it, Reverend Grabowski heard me. And in the next few minutes I learned what the word blasphemy meant. I've never, ever forgotten that lecture, even to this day. Mother was very embarrassed when Reverend Grabowski told her later, and I was severely reprimanded at home also.

The rest of the classes were uneventful and after confirmation Sunday was over, Mother had the relatives out to our farm house for dinner. It was a great day. Everyone congratulated me and, best of all, brought presents! Among the gifts and cards were a few dollars I could add to my bicycle fund. That made me very happy.

Then there was the end of Country School. There were only three of us in the eighth grade that year, out of a total of about twenty four in all the grades. Our teacher, Mrs. Steinbach, planned a farewell party

Confirmation day.

for the three of us who were going on to High School in the fall. She asked the two other older boys and me if we would sing a song at the party. I was a little reluctant at first, but the other two boys said they would, so I agreed also.

I might not have accepted that invitation if it hadn't been for the opportunity I'd had that spring to participate in a sing-along in Hill Auditorium at the University of Michigan. Earlier in the year, a music teacher had visited each of the country schools in the county to teach us all a little bit about choral singing. My voice, like that of a couple of the other boys, was beginning to change, but we were still invited to participate in the enormous children's choir at the May Festival.

The University of Michigan sent out busses to pick up all of us country school children and bring us to Hill Auditorium. When we arrived, there were ushers to guide us up three long flights of stairs. We filled the entire third balcony! How amazing it was for us to take our seats and look way down to the main stage. It looked very small from where we sat. The song leader came on stage and stood beside a big piano, that didn't look big from where we were sitting, and the program began. The director motioned for all of us up in the balcony to rise and, with the piano accompanying us, we sang our hearts out. We sang a few simple folk songs from around the world, and I knew I'd never forget that day.

The Country School party was a fun time. The three of us boys sang, "Old MacDonald Had A Farm." My voice had changed enough to sing baritone, the other two boys sang bass and tenor. It went well, everyone said, but though I continued to sing in church, I never again sang as a soloist, or in a small group program.

After the party, and the many fond farewells that passed among us students, Mrs. Steinbach, and the parents who were there, my summer vacation started.

Summer vacation always meant that it was off with my shoes and socks and running barefoot again. I didn't realize it then, but this was going to be the last summer I would go barefoot. With High School coming in the fall, my lifestyle would change dramatically.

But that summer I still helped Father by getting the cows from pasture, milking, and cooling the milk. I also helped with caring for our farm animals, putting in the corn, cultivating, making hay, harvesting the wheat and threshing.

And I earned the rest of the money I needed to buy a bicycle. I'd been saving for it for years. I knew just the one I wanted. I saw a picture of it in a Montgomery Ward Department store ad in the Ann Arbor News. It was thirty five dollars, a lot of money in the nineteen thirties.

But Grandfather had a good crop of strawberries and raspberries that year and by the end of the berry season, and with Father offering to make up the difference, I had enough money saved.

So, one day after morning chores and dinner, Father and I changed out of our farm clothes and we drove to Ann Arbor on US 12. When we got downtown we turned right on Main Street. (Even then, there were lots of cars parked along both sides of the street.) A couple of blocks down we found a parking space almost right in front of the Montgomery Ward store. I was out the door before Father even shut off the engine.

When we stepped into Montgomery Ward, I stopped and stood wide eyed at the sight of that enormous store, full of items for sale. I had never seen anything like that before! But, after a minute, I grabbed Father's arm and asked him where the bicycles might be. He said we'd ask a salesman. We did and were directed to an aisle on our left. Hurrying, pulling Father along, I paid little attention to the other things on display—it was the bike I was interested in. When I finally spotted them I just stood in awe at the sight before me. Finally, letting go of Father's arm, I started mingling among all those bikes, wondering how I would decide which was the one for me.

But, it didn't take me long. There it was. Painted bright red, with white stripes on the top of the fenders, shiny chrome handlebars and balloon tires—what more could I want? I checked the price tag—yes, it was thirty five dollars.

By now a clerk was at our side and the deal was made. I eagerly pushed the bike down the aisle, out the door, and to our car. Father helped me put it in the back seat.

The drive home seemed to take forever. I couldn't wait to have my first ride on that beautiful machine! When we finally arrived and drove up the driveway, Father blew the horn and everyone came out of the house. I again jumped out before he even stopped. Father got the bike out of the back seat and stood it on its wheels. I immediately climbed aboard and pedaled down the driveway. What a thrill that first ride was! Marjorie begged me to let her ride too. I worried that she was

100

too young and small, but I helped her get on, held the seat and let her take a short ride.

For the rest of that afternoon I rode up and down the driveway and all over the yard, until Father reminded me it was time to get the cows in. I reluctantly put the bike in our woodshed, changed back into my farm clothes and headed for the pasture field. All I could think about was that now I would get to ride my bike every day.

****

On the left is Alex, my partner in crime, the first and only time I tried smoking.

Then there was the time I tried smoking.

We had new neighbors that summer. A family bought the old farmhouse across the highway from our barn. They had two kids, Alex and Helen, both a little younger than me. They often came to play with Marjorie, Lloyd and me at our house. One day we were playing around in the new wheat from that summer's crop. Alex and Helen were from the city and had never played in a granary filled with freshly threshed wheat. They really enjoyed it. They told us this would be their first year in a country school. I told them that soon I would be going to high school for the first time. Helen replied, "In high school, some of the older students even smoke and drink beer!" She had seen them do it.

This was news to me. I had never thought about things like that.

After they returned home, as Marjorie, Lloyd and I left the barn, heading for the house, I couldn't forget what Helen said about the smoking, and even drinking, in the high school in the city where they had lived. I began to worry about my high school. "No, that couldn't be going on there," I thought as we went inside for our noon meal.

After dinner Father suggested maybe I could mow the lawn. So, I went to the woodshed where our red push-type mower was stored, and started mowing. While I was cutting the lawn, my mind wandered back to the conversation with our new friends, especially what Helen said about drinking and smoking in the city's high school.

After an hour of mowing in the warm summer afternoon, I felt like I needed a rest. I looked across the highway and saw Alex playing in his front yard. Suddenly an idea came into my head. I remembered he had said his father smoked cigarettes. My father only smoked an occasional cigar, which didn't intrigue me. But cigarettes!

I had seen ads in magazines where wild west cowboys made their own cigarettes by rolling some ground tobacco in little pieces of white paper, and then lighting them up and taking puffs with happy looks on their faces. I thought maybe I should try it.

Looking across the highway at Alex, I decided I needed a little support from someone to carry out the idea that was now in my mind. So, I went into the house where Mother was finishing getting the house in order after dinner, and asked her if I could take a break from mowing the lawn and go over to the old house and see Alex for a little while. She said, "Yes, but don't stay too long."

Before leaving the house I went to the basement. Near the furnace Father kept a box of matches on a shelf. I took a few and put them in my pocket. Then I remembered I needed some paper to make a cigarette. I found a piece on a table nearby, grabbed it and ran up the stairs, out the back door and down the driveway over to where Alex was playing in his yard.

We sat down, leaning against a tree, and in a rather excited voice I told him I was interested in this smoking we had talked about that morning. Since I would be going to high school soon, maybe I should try it before school starts. I told him I had matches and a piece of paper and all I needed was something to use for tobacco. On the way over to Alex's house I had noticed some weeds growing along the fence that had gone to seed. The seeds looked just the color and texture of tobacco.

Alex was agreeable and we got up and headed over to the fence. I grabbed the top of the weed with both hands and stripped the nice brown seeds off the stem and into my hands—at least a cupful. I put the seeds in my pocket and we went out back of an old storage shed, where nobody could see us, and I got out the matches and piece of paper. I quickly shaped the paper so it would hold the seeds, laid some on it and rolled it into the shape of a cigarette.

Now to light it! Alex found a small stone to scratch the match on and with the imitation cigarette between my lips, I struck the match, lit the end of the cigarette and drew a strong inward breath.

I thought the world was coming to an end. My nose and throat felt like they were on fire. I coughed and, according to Alex who was watching in amazement, started laughing. He said smoke was coming out of my nose, ears and even my eyes. It felt like it.

In a couple of minutes things cleared up and I saw the remains of the cigarette laying at my feet. I stomped on it and vowed I would never try smoking again. (And, I never did.)

I then hurried back home, went into the well house where we cooled the milk, and washed my hands and face with water from the well pump, so Mother wouldn't catch on to what I had done.

What about the drinking of beer, that Alex's sister, Helen mentioned? Well, it turns out that by that time I had already decided that beer wasn't for me either.

The annual Schairer family reunion was held every June at my grandparents' house. All the families were of German descent and good cold beer was expected to be available. Grandfather was not a believer in the drinking of alcoholic beverages, but that did not mean the rest of the guests felt as he did. So he always purchased a supply of beer and pop at the corner store.

I happened to visit him one time in June, just when he arrived home from the store with those supplies. As he was putting the refreshments in the new, electric refrigerator, the first one my grandparents ever had, he looked at me and asked if I would like to try a little beer. "Sure," I said. I think he knew I wouldn't like it.

103

He poured a small amount in a glass and handed it to me. I eagerly raised the glass to my lips, took a big sip, and swallowed. The reaction of my taste buds was almost the same as when I later tried smoking. I looked at Grandfather and said, "I don't like it." I never tried beer again. It sure saved me a lot of money over the years.

****

I also vividly recall the day I first rode my bike to the High School in Dexter. It was the Sunday of Labor Day weekend. During breakfast, after the morning chores, Father suggested that maybe I should make a trial run on my bike over to the High School. We would do this after going to church and a quick Sunday dinner. I was excited. Church and Sunday school just dragged that day. I wanted the morning to go faster. The drive home seemed to take forever! I asked Mother if she could hurry the dinner along when we got home, so we could get an early start on the trip to the High School. She said she would try.

She kept her promise and by two o'clock we were ready to roll. Father told me to get a head start on my bicycle and they would come along in the car a little later and catch up with me. I had changed into casual clothes before dinner, so I'd be more comfortable riding my bike.

With a quick goodbye, I rushed out the door to the woodshed, wheeled out my bike, jumped on and headed down the driveway and lane to Parker road. There I turned right and traveled north toward Dexter and the High School.

It was a nice afternoon, not too warm, just right for a bike ride. The grass and the small bushes growing along the sides of the road showed the signs of a hot, dry summer, and the bike tires stirred up

Dexter High School., the way it looked when I went to school there.

dust as I pedaled down the gravel road. I rode down the hill towards the bridge that crossed Mill Creek where Grandfather and I fished, and where Marjorie, Lloyd and I went swimming now and then.

About a mile from home I passed a neighbor's farm where they had some dairy cows. Some of them were looking for grass to eat, while others were laying in the shade of a nearby tree. A little further on, the road passed through a large wood lot, with huge trees on either side of the road. It was darker and cooler as I pedaled through the opening in the trees.

I turned right onto Shield Road, the side road leading to Baker Road, the main road into Dexter. About halfway to Baker, I crossed another bridge over Mill Creek. That creek wound around and eventually ended in Mill Creek Pond on the west side of Dexter.

When I came to Baker Road I turned left toward town and the High School. There were only a few houses along Baker Road on the outskirts of town, but the first one I came to always made me nervous. I remembered the dog there. Pedaling along, thinking about what was ahead for me, sure enough, I heard the barking of that dog. And there he was, running down the driveway towards the road, a medium sized brown and white mutt, fully intent on attacking this "thing", me, coming down the road.

What do I do now? Gathering my thoughts quickly, I decided to pedal really fast and then put my feet up on the handlebars, alongside my hands, and coast by the dog, because I figured it was my moving legs it was after.

It worked, because it ran alongside the fast moving bike and couldn't reach my feet and legs, so he stopped and returned back to his driveway. Lucky me! I continued on my way.

By this time my folks had caught up with me. They passed me and stopped by the side of the road. Father said he would lead from here and that I should follow him to the home of a friend of his, near the school, where I would be able to leave my bike while I was in school.

We turned right onto Grand Street. This street was uphill all the way to the school. Father finally turned into a driveway just three houses from the school. Was I ever glad! I was becoming exhausted. This was the house of the Zeiglers, who owned a good, old fashioned German meat market in Dexter.

Attached to the front of their home was a beautiful stone porch. We all gathered there for a while and visited. Both the Zeiglers had a distinct German accent. They told me that I could leave my bike at their house during school hours and they would watch it for me. This appealed to me because I sure didn't want anyone stealing it.

After we visited for a little, Father said it was almost chore time again and he and Mother, Marjorie and Lloyd piled back in our car and headed home. I said a final thank you and goodbye to the Zeiglers, jumped on my bike and started back. Going down Grand Street was a lot more fun than coming up because I could coast all the way to Baker Road. Turning left, I pedaled towards home.

The trip back was uneventful. I saw the occasional squirrel, carrying a large nut in its mouth from the walnut trees growing along the road. Putting up their winter supply. I also, now and then, met a car heading for town. Folks who had been out visiting relatives and friends that Sunday.

As I pedaled through the opening in the woods on Parker Road in the late afternoon sunshine, I noticed the leaves on some of the maple trees showing signs of the fall colors that would soon to be adorning them.

I crossed the old Mill Creek bridge and when I turned left into the farm lane, heading for the house, I saw that I was back in time to get the cows from pasture.

I put the bike in the woodshed, hurried into our house and quickly changed into a work shirt and my bib overalls. Of course, I also took off the shoes I had worn all day—it was Sunday after all—and headed for the barn yard. As I passed the barn, I hollered to Father that I would get the cows.

I headed down the lane, and the dry, dusty dirt in the path puffed up between my barefoot toes. It still felt just as good as it had for many years.

Once the cows were in the barn yard and I closed the lane gate behind them, an ominous thought crossed my mind. Tomorrow I probably could get the cows again in my bare feet, but when I start High School I will have to wear shoes. Will that mean these wonderful moments will end? When I entered the barn, Father, perhaps noticing my worried expression, said that I have had a long day and that he would finish the chores and milking so I can go to the house and rest a bit.

I gladly accepted his offer, thanked him and hurried to the house. I washed my dusty feet at the well house and then headed to the front porch where Mother, Marjorie and Lloyd were enjoying the last of the late summer evening. I sat on the cement topped stone wall of the porch, with my bare feet dangling over the edge, and again that same worry crossed my mind. Was this the last of my "barefoot boy with cheeks of tan" days? Turns out it was. After the next day, those wonderful days were over forever. Except for the beautiful memories.

****

I find it difficult to pull up many exciting memories of my high school days. There were memorable events to be sure, but my memories of those years are not as vivid as those of my country school days.

Of course, I always enjoyed the bike ride to school on nice spring and fall days. In the winter though, I was fortunate to be able to get there in an automobile. Either Father or Mother drove me, or I caught a ride with Grace and Irene Parker. Mr. Parker was the neighbor farmer who buzzed our wood. His daughter Grace was two years older than I, and could drive her father's car to school.

For me, coming from tiny Country School, Dexter High was a big town school with lots of students. Many times in the first few weeks of school my thoughts flashed back to what they said about smoking and drinking in the city schools. But, I didn't see any of that in my first few years at Dexter High. In the later years I remember that one of my classmates, Fred Binder, did bring to school a little jar of homemade wine that his uncle had made. I tried it, but it didn't taste good to me.

After a few weeks I became adjusted to the routine of High School classes, the teachers, and the general environment. There were very few extracurricular activities in those days, no basketball, soccer or tennis. There was some baseball and football, but even those were played on farmers' fields not far from the school. And besides, for me, though I never had to do morning chores on school days, the usual farm chores were ever present after school.

I tried out for baseball, but weighing in at one hundred and thirty pounds and only five foot eight, I soon discovered I wasn't equipped physically for baseball, and certainly not for football. A new auditorium was built during my junior year, complete with a stage and a basketball court. But basketball and theater weren't for me either. Truth is, I was always ready to get back to the farm after school ended for the day.

I do remember a few highlights from my high school days. Near the end of my freshman year, I won a contest in my literature class by reciting a scene from a Shakespeare play. I received a fountain pen for my efforts. I think I surprised the teacher, as well as my classmates, that I actually got up in front of the class for my presentation. I think I even surprised myself.

I enjoyed those literature classes as much as any others, except maybe typing, which was easy for me, and physics and chemistry. My literature teacher Miss Josephine Crocker is still alive as I write this in 2008, and living in the nursing home here at the Chelsea Retirement Community where Jane and I also live. She graduated from Dexter High in 1927 and has been a single lady all her life. I graduated in 1939. That's almost seventy years ago. I find that very hard to believe.

As time went by, I garnered close friendships with several other boys in my class, most of them fellow farm boys from the area. A couple of them had cars of their own. Over lunch hour, we all brought our own lunches, we would gather together in one of the cars to en-joy them. Sometimes after eating, a couple of the boys brought out cigarettes to puff on. My friend Floyd Evinger was the biggest smok-er. Occasionally they came up with a couple of cigars and lit them and filled the cars with so much smoke that we couldn't see out the windows! This brought back for me those horrible moments of the only time I tried smoking before high school. Those smoke filled cars cemented my thinking that I would never succumb to the smoking habit.

Not all of our noon lunches were like that. Occasionally we would ride out of town and stop along the Huron River, under a few trees, and watch the water run by as we ate. Sometimes we barely made it back to school for the afternoon sessions.

There were twenty five classmates in my graduating class and we were about equally divided in number between boys and girls. I never became "attached" to any one of the girls, but got along with them all through those high school days. A couple of them were very good students and a few of us farm boys managed to get answers to some hard class questions now and then. I particularly remember Jeanette Bates. Her father, Carl, was president of the school board.

I found Chemistry class very interesting. We had a very liberal minded teacher, Mr. Carl Place. Mr. Place was almost like one of us boys in class. My friend, Fred Binder, and I got together on projects now and then, like making gunpowder to make our own fireworks. One time we even tried to make nitroglycerine! Over a noon hour we took a test tube full of this liquid out in the country and threw it against a big rock along the road. Thank the Lord, nothing happened. We went back to school somewhat disappointed. But, we never tried it again.

****

My junior year of high school, 1937-1938, came to an end on the first of June. I was looking forward to the summer vacation time. In September I would be starting my senior year. But, I wasn't thinking about that then. Believe it or not, I was really looking forward to helping Father with the summer farm work again. Also to fun summer pastimes like neighborhood baseball and swimming in the old swimming hole down at the creek on hot evenings after a hard day's work.

Just before school was over, three of my classmates, Fred, Jim and Lawrence (we called him Zig, a nickname from his last name) conjured up the idea of taking a short vacation as soon as school was out and before we started helping with the farm work. Jim did not live on a farm, but was country oriented, since his family lived just outside the town of Dexter. He had a driver's license and access to his father's car for such a trip.

None of us had ever been to a big city. We had heard all kinds of stories about what went on there and we decided we'd go to Chicago! I was the youngest. I was only sixteen and wouldn't be seventeen until the following January. The other three boys were already seventeen and would be eighteen by the time they graduated.

Father and Mother were a bit reluctant to have me take this trip to a "Big City," but realized that maybe I was now old enough to know what I was doing. They eventually relented and accepted the fact that I would be on my first trip without them to watch over me.

My friends and I decided we'd go the first weekend of June, right after school was out. That Thursday evening I packed a few clothes in a small suitcase so I'd be ready to leave the next day for Chicago. I remember I didn't sleep very much that night. The next morning I got up early and helped Father with a few morning chores. I'd just finished breakfast when a car horn sounded out in the driveway. I jumped up from my chair and, with a hasty goodbye to my family, I bounded out the back door, suitcase in hand, and joined my friends waiting for me in Jim's family's 1936 Buick. We started out the driveway, across the streetcar tracks, and turned west on the two lane concrete highway, then known as U.S. 12, on our way to Chicago.

It was about nine in the morning. It would be a two hundred and fifty mile drive. We wanted to be in Chicago by late afternoon, hopefully before dark. We would have to pass through a number of small towns, as well as a couple of larger ones, Battle Creek and Kalamazoo.

Traffic was not very heavy. We cruised along at fifty five miles an hour, occasionally passing a streetcar on the tracks that ran along the highway. The streetcar stopped at the depot in Jackson, and at some of the other small towns. We saw many cows and sheep grazing in pasture fields along the highway, and farmers in the fields, planting corn.

There weren't many homes along the highway then; mostly fields and the occasional farm houses.

We passed through Battle Creek and I remember a big sign pointing the way to a veterans cemetery just outside of town. On the outskirts of Kalamazoo we stopped for a bite to eat and picked up gas for the car. Gas cost twenty cents a gallon then.

In the Kalamazoo River area, farming changed to large celery and vegetable fields. A beautiful sight indeed. By the middle of the afternoon we were fast approaching the last of Michigan, and headed into Illinois and Chicago—the Big City.

When we entered the city limits the traffic increased. Approaching the downtown area, we came upon a main cross street. As Jim was about to enter the intersection, the traffic light turned yellow. He instantly applied the brakes and came to a stop right in the middle of the intersection. Horns began blowing from all directions, and a policeman came running to the driver's side of our car. Jim, and all of us, were petrified. It was a warm day, Jim had his window down, and the officer shouted to him that he should never stop in the middle of an intersection on a yellow light. He motioned for him to get going, which he did.

We decided that it had been a long day and maybe we should find a place to stay for the night and relax. Earlier along the way, we'd agreed that we would look for a nice, fancy downtown hotel in which to spend our couple of nights in the Big City.

A few blocks from that intersection we spotted a big sign directing us to a hotel just a little way further along, on our side of the street. From the outside, it looked just like what we had been thinking about and so we pulled off the street right into the hotel parking lot.

We were optimistic that this was where we would spend the night, so we grabbed our luggage and headed for the front door . When we entered the lobby we were overwhelmed by the sight before us. Bright lights shone from all the walls of the hallways and from the ceilings. There were a number of well dressed people on the mezzanine floor, a few feet higher than the main entrance and lobby where we entered. We began wondering if the hotel clerk at the lobby counter would

I did learn to play the piano, and have enjoyed playing it all my life. This photo was taken in 2006, when I was 84 years old.

even let us country boys stay there. But, a well dressed lady behind the counter greeted us with a smile and took our hard earned money for a couple of nights' stay at this beautiful hotel.

With luggage in hand, we walked along a short hall to a four-step stairway up to a living room-like area. As we walked towards the steps I heard a piano being played. A well dressed man was at a big grand piano. I had to stop and listen. I was really struck by the sound of the music he was playing. I had been taking piano lessons for the past year and this man's playing really stimulated my desire to learn to play the piano like that.

We continued down the hall to an elevator—first time any of us had ever been in one—and rode it up to our floor. We found our room, unlocked the door, and entered a large, bright colored room with two double beds waiting for us four tired young country boys. This would be great! But, we were also hungry from our day's traveling and had noticed the hotel dining room on the way to our room. We put our luggage on the floor, sat on the edge of the beds to try them for comfort, and then hurried back to the dining room for supper.

We enjoyed a fancy meal, the likes of which we had never had before. It was expensive, but being waited on by these well dressed waiters made it worth the cost. This was the Big City! After finishing our dinner, being tired, we went back to our room. It didn't take long and we were ready to try those hotel beds, two of us to a bed, and were soon fast asleep. It had been a full day and tomorrow we would explore the city.

And that we did! We walked all over the streets of downtown Chicago. As we looked up at the tall skyscrapers, we could almost hear the local folks whisper, "Oh, they are just some country boys." We visited a museum and I remember seeing skeletons of some animals there. In the late afternoon we made our way back to the hotel. Once again as we entered the hotel lobby I could hear that piano playing coming from the mezzanine floor above. The same man again sat at the keyboard. I listened for a time and again thought that I wanted to learn to be able to do that.

We were very tired from our long day exploring the Big City and, after another dinner in the dining room, we went to our room and immediately to bed.

The next morning we were up and out of the hotel and on our way home by eight o'clock. We had seen the Big City and decided it wasn't for us.

The drive home was uneventful. Fred and I rode in the back seat. As we were traveling along we talked some about what we had experienced the day before. I know I fell asleep now and then. We drove into my folks' driveway about six o'clock that evening and, grabbing my luggage, I bid the other boys goodbye and hurried into the farm house. Mother, Marjorie and Lloyd were waiting to greet me. Father had gone to the barn to milk the cows. I was back with my family in my familiar, comfortable setting, but I never would forget that trip to the Big City.

****

Toward the end of our senior year, our class took a trip to Washington D.C. We went on a Blue Goose Bus Line tour bus, all twenty-five of us seniors, and saw many of the famous Washington landmarks. We toured the White House, the Capitol and walked up all the stairs to the top of the Washington Monument and looked out the windows over the city.

As the final year drew to a close, we approached graduation. Every class was asked to provide something for the ceremony. My class was asked to provide the closing element for the program. We decided that our chemistry class should provide a rousing finale to the afternoon affair. What did we come up with? The class asked Fred Binder and me, he was the friend who worked with me on the nitro, to come up with some kind of a small fireworks display for the conclusion. This was all to happen inside the auditorium, on the stage up front.

Fred and I came up with the idea of making about a quart of gunpowder. We knew that by mixing a small amount of certain other chemicals with the gunpowder base, we could create different colors as it burned. Copper sulfate would create a blue color, Strontium Nitrate red, while gunpowder burns almost white. The colors in the American flag. What an ending for the afternoon's program! And yes, believe it or not, we got permission from our chemistry teacher, Mr. Place, to actually go through with this plan!

Fred and I made up the mixture of gunpowder and chemicals the morning of the big day. We got the custodian to put an eight foot folding table at the back of the stage for us to use. We brought the powder from the classroom, along with a narrow metal strip to put the powder on, so as not to burn the table. With the metal strip in place, we carefully poured a small amount of the gunpowder along the length of the metal strip, then mixed a small amount of the other two chemicals every few inches along the way, so we'd have a series of red, white and blue flashes to create the effect of a great American flag.

In the afternoon, the program started with the other classes doing their presentations. Then came our turn. Fred and I moved the table from the back of the stage to the front edge, so everyone could see. Fred took out a match and as I stood back, he struck it and lit a short little strip of paper that acted as a fuse to light the powder. After he lit the fuse, Fred jumped back from the table.

I never saw anything like it, before or since. Everything went off just as we planned, only more. It only took a few seconds for the gunpowder to burn off across the table and create a series of colorful red, white and blue flashes as it burned. But, the burning powder also created a huge cloud of black smoke that enveloped the entire auditorium. The whole place emptied very quickly. Fred and I received no repercussions from the stunt but, to the best of my knowledge, it was never tried again.

Then school was over for the summer. Fred and I hurried back to the chemistry room. I grabbed a couple of my books to take home, headed out the main door, across the street to the house where my bike was parked, pushed it to the street and jumped on. I coasted down the hill to Baker Road and headed for home as fast as I could. I made it back to the farm the fastest ever that afternoon. When I arrived home I parked the bike against the wall of the house, grabbed my books from the bike basket and ran inside. Mother was in the kitchen when I came in. I tossed the books on the table and said, "That's the last of school for me."

And it was. I stayed on the farm and worked it with Father from then on.

My brother Lloyd and my sister Marjorie both had the opportunity to go to high school in Ann Arbor. A generous neighbor of my folks worked at the University of Michigan and their time schedules coincided. For four years they had transportation to and from high school, much to the delight of my folks. Both of them went on to the U.M. and graduated. Lloyd received a degree in botany. Maybe a bit of the farmer genes were in his blood too. Marjorie later married a classmate of hers who was from Oklahoma, and moved there with him to raise a family. Lloyd secured a job in Long Island at the Brookhaven

Me, Marjorie and Lloyd, probably on Marjorie's graduation from High school. Note how the trees have grown up around our house.

National Laboratories. He married a Long Island girl and also raised a family.

I want to end my story by telling of the unexpected honor I received from Dexter High School fifty years after I graduated. I got a call one day and the caller said I had been selected for the Dexter High School Hall of Fame.

115

Jane, me, Grandfather Jacob, Lloyd (graduating from the U of M), my father and mother.

He hoped I could be present to accept this award. After catching my breath, I assured him that Jane and I would be at the Alumni Banquet to receive this honor. To this very day I wonder what I did through the years to deserve this. It is an honor I really cherish. To be placed in the Hall of Fame among other former graduates is truly heart warming for me.

Today my picture hangs on the wall of the main entrance of the recently built new Dexter High School. The new school is just two miles from our old farm. I used to pedal my bike past the land it sits on when I bicycled to the old school almost seventy years ago!

Made in the USA
Charleston, SC
13 October 2011